ADOBE FIREWORKS CS4
HOW-TOs
100 ESSENTIAL TECHNIQUES

JIM BABBAGE

Adobe Fireworks CS4 How-tos
100 Essential Techniques

Jim Babbage

This Adobe Press book is published by
Peachpit.

Peachpit
1249 Eighth Street
Berkeley, CA 94710
510/524-2178
510/524-2221 (fax)

Peachpit is a division of Pearson Education.

For the latest on Adobe Press books, go to
www.adobepress.com

To report errors, please send a note to errata@peachpit.com

Acquisitions Editor: Pam Pfiffner
Project Editor: Susan Rimerman
Developmental Editor: Anne Marie Walker
Technical Editor: Kim Cavanaugh
Production Editor: Tracey Croom
Composition: ICC MacMillan Inc.
Indexer: James Minkin
Cover and Interior Design: Mimi Heft

ISBN 13: 978-0-321-56287-6

ISBN 10: 0-321-56287-9

9 8 7 6 5 4 3 2 1

Printed and bound in the United States of America

Dedication

To the memory of my first and best teacher, my dad Barry Babbage, who taught me, among many other things, to always find time to do the things you love. Miss ya, Dad, every day.

Acknowledgments

Working in this industry, I learned long ago that you don't exist in a vacuum. I am surrounded by friends, family, and colleagues who have helped me "get through" and stay grounded during the writing of this book.

I'm grateful for the support and patience of many friends and family members too numerous to mention without fear of leaving someone out. But a special thanks goes to friend and fellow author Tom Green for his counsel and his ability to make me laugh at anything, including myself.

Thanks to Ray West, and Community MX, who got me started on this wild and crazy ride, and helped me in no small way to establish a name and reputation for myself.

Thanks to my team at Peachpit, Susan Rimerman, Anne Marie Walker, and Tracey Croom, for keeping things on track, and especially to my technical editor and friend Kim Cavanaugh who had many sage words of advice during the creation of this book.

Contents

CHAPTER ONE

Getting Started

The question I hear most often from the uninitiated is: What is Fireworks? My answer varies, but in a nutshell, Fireworks is a hybrid imaging application that combines vector and bitmap imaging technologies and techniques in a single graphics application. Its unique approach to imaging is due to the specific focus of Fireworks, which is creating and manipulating screen graphics for the Web or for other screen-based tools such as Power-Point or Flash. Fireworks is a creative and professional production tool that lets you quickly and easily create, edit, or alter graphics and designs.

Fireworks can save you a valuable commodity—time—which there never seems to be enough of in today's fast-paced, demanding digital world. Not to mention, Fireworks is a blast. It makes your production work fun.

One of the original goals of the Fireworks development team was to create a program in which users could do all their work without ever having to jump to another application. The built-in flexibility of Fireworks and its "everything is editable all the time" mandate have been present since version 1. If my visuals are destined for the screen, Fireworks is my program of choice.

With the release of Adobe Fireworks CS4, the program has gained even more distinction as a unique application for *rapid prototyping* through the introduction of a new *pages* feature as well as the ability to easily build interface components for Flex applications. Another new feature is Rich Symbols, which allows you to create UI elements and even add in additional "states" without having to go any further than a dialog box.

Improved—or completely new—integration with many of the original stable of Adobe products such as Photoshop, Illustrator, and Bridge enables Fireworks designers to accept and open files in several formats without having to request special "treatment" from the originator of the artwork.

Fireworks can be even further extended by those skilled in JavaScript or Flash. Productivity enhancements can be created by the end user, making Fireworks an application that can be set up to work the way you want it to.

In the end, it's all about choice—intelligent and experienced decisions based on using the software. The right tool for the right job, as they say.

That's where this book comes in. Each chapter contains tips or techniques that can help you be more productive in Fireworks. There is no need to read the book in a linear fashion, cover to cover. To make things a bit easier, I have focused on specific topic areas: the workspace (Chapters 1, 2, 3, 4, 6, 9, 10, and 12), working with text (Chapter 7), and work flow integration (Chapters 5, 8, 10, 11, and 13).

Jump in wherever you want. I hope you have as much fun as I do working with Fireworks CS4.

#1 Creating a New Document

The Document window is where the magic happens, from editing an existing image to creating your own original Web page comp.

Creating a new, empty document from the Welcome Screen is as simple as clicking on the Fireworks Document (PNG) item. You can also create a new document by pressing Ctrl/Command1+N.

The New Document dialog displays, allowing you to set the dimensions for your new file as well as the resolution and canvas color (**Figure 1**). The default canvas color is white, but you can choose Transparent or select a custom color.

If you opt for a custom color, a color picker appears onscreen when you click the color box just below the word Custom.

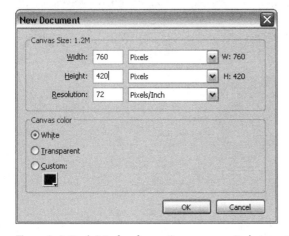

Figure 1 A simple interface for creating a new, empty document.

When you have made all your decisions, just click OK and the Welcome Screen will disappear and be replaced by your new, blank document.

Help Yourself to Help

Like most software applications, there is always a learning curve. Constant practice and experience will aid you in becoming more proficient, but it's always good to know that help is not far away. You can access the Fireworks Help files by selecting the Help menu or by pressing F1.

Choosing the main Fireworks Help menu item launches the Adobe Help Viewer, where you can browse or search for help on the topic of your choice. Adobe Help Viewer let's you search by keyword or phrase, as well as browse Help chapters.

The main Help menu also gives you quick access to the Adobe User Forums, as well as the Fireworks Support, Developer, and Documentation Resource centers located on the Adobe Web site. An Internet connection is needed to access these options.

#2 It's All About the Pixels

Resolution and the Web

Pixels per inch (ppi) is a unit of measure relative only to the print world. When dealing with screen graphics, your concern should be the *pixel dimensions* (640 x 480, 760 x 420, etc.). The default resolution Fireworks begins with is 96 ppi and it can be left as it is. If you are planning to use Fireworks for a print project, you will need to be concerned with ppi. A general guideline is 300 ppi. Be aware, however, that Fireworks is best at creating images meant to be viewed on a computer screen, not graphics intended for the printed page. Fireworks does not recognize CMYK color' or printer profiles, so your end result may not print accurately.

On the plus side, Fireworks now supports PDF export, so printing your designs has become a bit easier. More on this in Chapter 2, "Graphics Boot Camp."

Fireworks is first and foremost a screen graphics editor. Your computer monitor displays content by using pixels, so it's only natural that Fireworks is best suited for handling graphics in this manner.

Fireworks CS4 doesn't recognize commercial printer color profiles or color modes such as CMYK (the ink colors used in commercial printing). And although you can create a document at a high resolution suitable for printing, such as 300 ppi, Fireworks is not truly optimized to work with these higher-quality files. This is most noticeable when you have several high-resolution files open at the same time.

Even though you can change the width and height settings to inches or centimeters, document rulers will only display in pixels. If your goal is to create graphics for print, it is generally recommended that you work with a more suitable program, such as Photoshop or Illustrator. In Fireworks, it's RGB and pixels all the way!

#3 Working with Tabbed Documents

Prior to CS4, the tabbed document feature was only available on Windows, but now it's on the Mac too. On both platforms Fireworks makes excellent use of tabs to organize the workspace and access open documents. When your documents are maximized within the document window, each file is represented by a tab. Clicking the tab makes the selected document active and editable (**Figure 3**).

Figure 3 Select the filename of any open document to bring it to the foreground.

The advantage to this feature is that you can maximize your workspace for the currently active document. There is no need to drag around various document windows, resize them, and so on. It's a much cleaner and clutter-free look.

If your documents are not maximized, tabs are not enabled, and you'll need to click and drag files to make them active or to position and resize them.

Mac View Options

If you're a Mac User, the new Adobe OWL interface with its unified application frame may be a surprise to you. Never fear, you have options. See Technique #76 to learn how to switch your application view to Classic mode on the Mac.

#4 Setting Up Rulers

The three traditional layout devices in Fireworks that help you position your various text and image objects within the currently open document are rulers, guides, and grids.

All these features are accessed from the View menu. You can show, hide, lock, clear, and turn on object snapping from this menu.

Although it's not a default setting, it's best to start your projects by displaying the rulers. With the rulers visible, the *x* and *y* position of your cursor will be visible as a solid, vertical and horizontal line within the ruler bars. As you move objects around the canvas with the cursor, you will also see the *x* and *y* locations of the object in the rulers. When you move an object, the lines change to solid bars that show exactly how much space the object uses on the rulers.

You can change the 0-axis for the rulers by dragging the zero point indicators with your cursor (**Figure 4**).

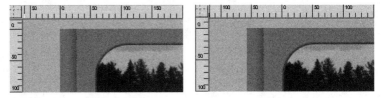

Figure 4 By dragging the crosshairs located in the upper-left corner of the rulers, you can reset the zero point of the rulers to any location on the canvas.

#5 Guides for Precise Layout

Guides can be used after the rulers are turned on. Simply click and drag from either the vertical or horizontal ruler to bring guides onto the canvas. Use guides to mark important parts of your document, such as the margins, the document center point, and areas where you want to work precisely. You can have as many guides on your canvas as you want. Their locations are entirely up to you.

Once on the canvas, you can reposition the guides by placing your cursor over the guide and waiting for the double-headed arrow icon to appear. Then just click and drag the guide to a new location (**Figure 5a**). Guides are represented by a bright green line.

Figure 5a Guide locations are easily changed using the mouse.

Note
Guides can be helpful when you want to align a series of objects or if you want to plan out how you will slice up your document for exporting Web graphics.

Remembering *X* and *Y*

If you have trouble remembering what *x* and *y* mean in terms of coordinates, this might help. Think of *x* as marking the position *across* the page (from left to right). Think of the vertical line of *y* as being *up and down*.

You can plan for several shapes that will become buttons in a Web page design. You can also drag out guides at specific intervals and snap those boxes to each guide, allowing for even vertical spacing and exact left alignment (**Figure 5b**).

Figure 5b You can snap image and text objects to guides to ensure accurate positioning.

#6 Using Grids

Grids give a graph-paper look to your canvas. You can customize the size of the grid, but you can't adjust individual gridlines like you can with guides.

You'll access grids from the View menu.

Like guides, a grid can be customized in terms of visibility, object snapping, and color, but because the grid is a set of lines designed to fill the canvas, you can also set the size of the grid.

If snapping is toggled on, not only will your objects snap to a grid intersection when you move close to the grid, but if you draw a shape or import a graphic, the cursor automatically snaps to the nearest gridlines while you drag the mouse (**Figure 6**).

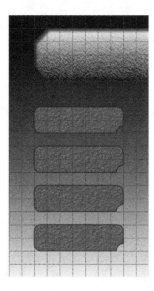

Figure 6 Objects can easily be aligned to each other using the grid, or they can be drawn to snap to the gridlines.

#7 Smart Guides and Tooltips

Along with the standard layout devices, Fireworks CS4 introduces two new layout devices: Smart Guides and Tooltips. Smart Guides display guides to help you align a selected object in relation to other objects on the canvas rather than just using guides or grids (**Figure 7a**). You can align a selected object based on vertical or horizontal centers and top, left, bottom, or right sides of the nearest object on the canvas.

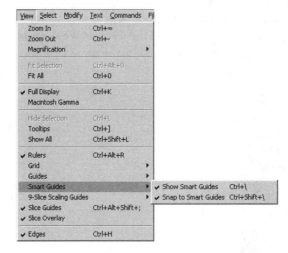

Figure 7a Accessed from the View menu, the new Smart Guides can help you position objects within the canvas area.

Unlike regular guides, Smart Guides are a live tool that will help you align objects even as you are drawing or resizing them.

If no other nearby image objects exist, Smart Guides will display as you move your object near the vertical or horizontal center of the canvas (**Figure 7b**).

Figure 7b Smart Guides let you align objects easily to the canvas or other objects while you move them.

9-Slice Scaling Guides

You might have noticed that 9-Slice Scaling Guides help you transform objects without distorting elements such as corner radii. More information on these guides is found in Chapter 4, "Staying on the (Vector) Path."

The bright green color of the guides will work in many situations, but there might be times when there is not enough contrast to separate the guides from your design.

By turning on Tooltips in the View menu, moving objects around the canvas also displays the *x/y* coordinates as a floating info box next to your cursor (**Figure 7c**). These coordinates are based on the Ruler settings. Keep in mind that if you change your 0 point on the rulers, the tooltip will take that into account when displaying the coordinates. Indeed, it will display negative values if your selected object is on the negative side of the 0 point.

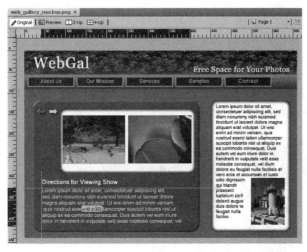

Figure 7c Activating Smart Guides, Rulers, and Tooltips provides you with many visual clues about the location and layout of your design.

Editing the Layout Tools

Editing attributes for the Rulers, Grids, Guides, Smart Guides, and 9-Slice Scaling is located in the Preferences dialog. You can change all editable attributes for each tool. You access Preferences by selecting Edit > Preferences (Windows) or by selecting Fireworks > Preferences (Mac).

Depending on your design, you may want to change the default color settings for these layout tools. The default colors are all hexadecimal values and are easy to change within the Preferences dialog:

- **Guides.** #00ffff
- **Grid.** #666666
- **Slice guides.** #ff4a4a
- **Smart guides.** #ff4aff
- **9-Slice scaling.** #0000ff

#8 Document Previews

Customizing the Panel View

Fireworks CS4 shares the same interface as other Creative Suite 4 products, making it easier to customize your panel arrangement. If you have used Fireworks in the past, Techniques 9–12 will orient you to the new way of working with panels.

Like most sophisticated programs, Fireworks uses panels to help you control attributes of selected objects and in some cases create *new objects*. Knowing your way around the panels and setting them up the way you want will speed up your workflow.

As you are working on your design, you can check anytime to see what an image will look like in a Web browser. Just above the document are four options, as shown in **Figure 8a**. By default, Fireworks opens files in the Original view, but you can change the view to Preview, 2-Up, or 4-Up to see how the browser will render your file based on the optimization settings in the Optimize panel or the Property Inspector.

Figure 8a While in Preview, 2-Up, or 4-Up views, you cannot edit the file, and all layout tools such as grids are hidden from view.

Optimization settings (file type, compression, and color settings) can be altered easily by choosing one of the optimization presets or by manually tweaking the settings to the desired values (**Figure 8b**). When you are in any view other than Original, changes to the Optimize panel will be reflected in the document window.

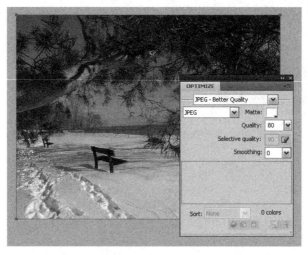

Figure 8b Optimization settings are easy to change using the Optimize panel, which is shown here separated from the main panel group.

If you want to see your image or design in a *real* browser, select File > Preview in Browser (**Figure 8c**) and choose a browser to launch. Fireworks will load your design into the browser using the current optimization settings. You can also set a default primary and secondary browser.

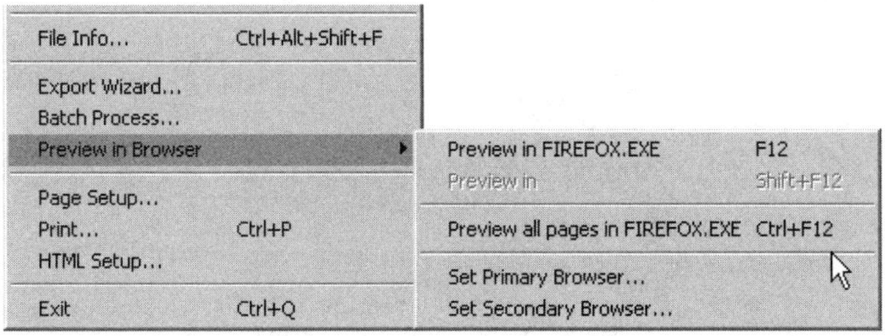

File Info...	Ctrl+Alt+Shift+F		
Export Wizard...			
Batch Process...			
Preview in Browser	▶	Preview in FIREFOX.EXE	F12
		Preview in	Shift+F12
Page Setup...		Preview all pages in FIREFOX.EXE	Ctrl+F12
Print...	Ctrl+P		
HTML Setup...		Set Primary Browser...	
Exit	Ctrl+Q	Set Secondary Browser...	

Figure 8c Preview in Browser.

For more details on the Optimize panel and exporting files for the Web, see Chapter 2, "Graphics Boot Camp" and Chapter 5, "Working with Multiple Images."

#9 Customizing the Panel Group

For Mac and Windows, panels are contained within a *panel* dock (**Figure9a**). You can view the panel dock in a variety of ways. It can be collapsed to an iconic mode or expanded to a traditional panel size with a single mouse click. You can also drag the panel dock to widen it. This makes the panel tabs within each panel group easier to read.

Showing and Hiding Panels

Fireworks has far more panels than there is screen real estate to display them, so if you're looking for a panel and can't find it, select the Window menu to activate it.

All Fireworks panels (including the toolbar and Property Inspector) can easily be displayed or hidden by pressing the Tab key. This is a quick way to maximize your screen space.

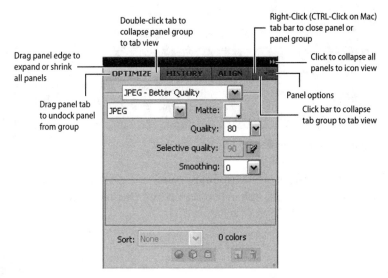

Figure 9a The panel dock and each panel group have a variety of controls.

If the panels are collapsed to iconic mode, clicking any icon will activate that specific panel group, making it fly out for access (**Figure 9b**). By default, if you click away from the panel group, it will collapse back to an icon. Personally, I find this annoying. You can change this behavior by right-clicking/Control-clicking at the top of the dock. A context menu appears, and you can deselect Auto-Collapse Icon Panels.

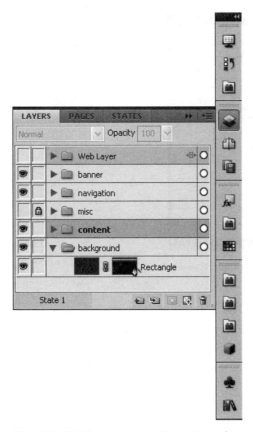

Figure 9b Clicking an icon in Icon view activates the selected panel group as a fly out.

#10 Panel Group Management

Many panels are grouped together in *panel groups*. For example, the Optimize and Align panels are in a panel group.

Panel groups can be collapsed to a Tab view (**Figure 10a**) or expanded by clicking the panel group title bar or the expansion icon in the upper-left corner of the panel. You can completely close a panel group by clicking the X icon in the upper-right corner of each group.

Figure 10a A compact view of panels in Tab view.

Tearing Off Panels

Dragging a panel tab away from the dock (referred to as tearing) converts the panel to a floating panel. Tearing a panel from the dock shifts the panel into a semitransparent state until you release the mouse. You can tear off any panel from the dock and drop it on the canvas.

Docking a Floating Panel

To re-dock a floating panel, click the panel tab or title bar and drag the panel back to the dock. Look for the highlight indicator to show you where the panel will be placed, and then release the mouse when you find a suitable location.

Most panels have a context-sensitive Options menu. The icon is located just below the close icon in each panel group. From this Options menu, you can perform various operations based on the currently active panel. **Figure 10b** shows the basics of panel management.

Changing the order of panels within a group has become *much* easier than it used to be. Simply drag a panel tab to reposition it within its current group, or drag it onto another group if you want to create a custom panel group.

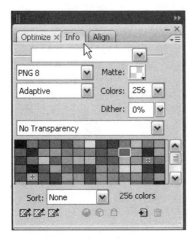

Figure 10b Drag a panel tab to reposition within the current group or drag to another group.

#11 Customizing the Workspace

Sometimes the default panel group settings will not be conducive to your workflow. I found this to be true with the Pages, Layers, Frames, and History panel groups. I prefer to be able to see the Pages and Layers panels at the same time rather than to have to toggle between them, because I want to know exactly where I am in my design at all times.

Fortunately, you can customize your workspace by creating new panel groups. For example, click on the Pages tab and drag the Pages tab between two panel groups. You will see a semitransparent version of the panel and a blue highlight bar (**Figure 11a**). Release the mouse and the Pages panel becomes its own group.

Figure 11a Tear off tabs or panels to float them in the workspace or to create new panel groups.

You can also move a panel and combine it with another group. Select a panel tab and click and drag the tab up to another panel group (**Figure 11b**). Panels can be in collapsed Tab view or expanded view when you move them. When the panel area is surrounded by a highlight, let go of the tab to create a custom panel group.

Figure 11b Customizing the panel group layout can be done many ways.

When the panels are set to your liking, save your new custom workspace by selecting Window > Workspace Layouts > Save Current (**Figure 11c**).

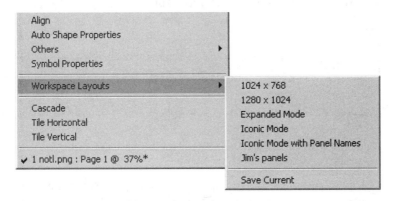

Figure 11c You can save your custom workspace, or workspaces.

#12 Modifying Tool Attributes

The Property Inspector is a context-sensitive panel. The controls within it change based on the currently selected tool or object on the canvas. It's technically just another panel, but it almost never gets turned off because its features are a core part of the application. It's worth noting that the Property Inspector is found throughout Fireworks, Dreamweaver, and Flash.

Select any tool in the toolbar and you will see the Property Inspector change to contain attributes for that specific tool. In **Figure 12a** the Blur tool is selected. The Property Inspector displays controls to change the size, edge shape, and intensity of the tool. You can enter numerical values or use the context sliders to alter the characteristics of the tool.

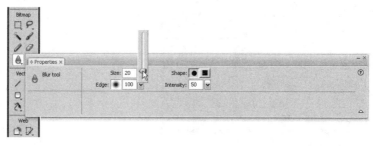

Figure 12a The Property Inspector does double duty, acting as a modifier for a selected tool or for a selected object.

With the Pointer tool, you can select an object on the canvas and the Property Inspector completely transforms to show you editable attributes of the currently selected object (**Figure 12b**).

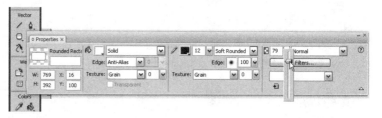

Figure 12b Different objects will have different editable properties. A selected vector object can be customized in many ways.

You can customize panel groups by adding any panels you want to the existing groups. You can now do this with the Property Inspector in CS4.

#13 The Joy of Multiple Undo

The last stop in this overview of the workspace is perhaps one of the most important workflow features in any creative application. It's been referred to as the Artist's Prerogative command and the Oh My Gawd command. In Fireworks, the Undo command is a keyboard command that let's you step back multiple times in the history of your document. By pressing Ctrl/Command+Z, you can step back at least 20 actions in the creation of your design. Pressing Ctrl/Command+Y steps you forward.

If 20 steps aren't enough for you to undo, you can access the Preferences dialog quickly by pressing Ctrl/Command+U and changing the Maximum Undos in the General category. You will have to restart Fireworks for this change to take effect. This is primarily a RAM-dependent decision because each history step must be stored in RAM while you work. If you don't have much RAM to spare, you might want to keep this number to a minimum.

When you close your file, the history steps are deleted.

The History Panel

Your changes are recorded in the History panel which can be accessed by pressing Shift+F10. If you find yourself doing the same tasks over and over again in a file (or multiple files), save your history steps as a custom command. You can then access the command anytime from the Commands menu. This can save you a lot of time and eliminate some of that necessary drudge work.

The History panel does not record mouse movements, so to create a complete custom command, use the keyboard commands and menu items.

To save a custom command, simply select all the steps you need in the History panel and press the small disc icon in the lower-right corner of the panel. You will be prompted for a name. Make it short but relevant because the name will appear in the Commands menu.

CHAPTER TWO

Graphics Boot Camp

Everyone knows the standard File > Open command, but Fireworks offers many more methods for opening images.

You can open files created in other applications or file formats, including Photoshop, FreeHand, Illustrator, uncompressed CorelDRAW, WBMP, EPS, JPEG, GIF, and animated GIF files. Camera RAW formats are not supported by Fireworks.

Many print design houses start Web page designs in Photoshop or Illustrator because those are the applications they are most comfortable with. The ability to reliably open Photoshop PSD and Illustrator AI files makes it easy to receive designs from other professionals in these common native formats and begin the Web workflow process.

When you open a file format other than Fireworks PNG using File > Open, you create a new Fireworks PNG document based on the original file. This puts all the Fireworks tools at your disposal. You edit the file and then either select Save As to save your work as a new Fireworks PNG file or as another file format. Depending on the work done to the file, or the file type, you can select Save to save the document in its original format. With the exception of the Photoshop PSD or Fireworks PNG formats, saving in the document's original format flattens the image to a single layer and eliminates your ability to edit the Fireworks-specific features you added to the image.

This chapter explores the ways in which you can get images into and out of Fireworks, including new and updated options. How you open, save, or export files depends on your goals with the image(s). In the end, knowing these techniques will help you choose the best method for your workflow.

#14 Opening Files with Adobe Bridge

Open as Untitled

If you're concerned about accidentally overwriting an original file, select the Open as "Untitled" check box in the main Open dialog. Your file will open as an untitled document, forcing you to name the file when you save it. The key of course is not to use the same filename when you save it!

Bridge is installed with the CS4 Suite or with most of the stand-alone applications in the suite. Using Bridge is part of my regular workflow. Not only can I see large versions of the images within Bridge, but I can even compare them side by side within the Bridge interface.

With Fireworks open, select File > Browse to open Adobe Bridge. You can search for files in a myriad of ways, but the two quickest ways are by using either the Favorites tab or the Folders tab. Favorites gives you quick access to commonly used folders and can be customized to show the folders you always use. The Folders tab acts like a mini file explorer and lets you drill down through your hard drive or external drives to find the folder you are looking for. When a folder is selected, its contents are displayed in the content area of Bridge.

Selecting an image brings up a large version of the thumbnail within the Preview pane. Holding down the Ctrl/Command key allows you to select additional images for the Preview pane so you can make comparisons. Multiple image selections in CS4 can bring up a *carousel* display—a pseudo 3-D interface that lets you twirl though the selected images. The carousel appears if there are more images selected than can be displayed in a "flat view" within the Preview pane. Keep in mind that all the tabs in Bridge can be adjusted in size by dragging the divider bars with the mouse.

You can hold down the Shift key to select multiple adjacent files as well.

When you have found the image you want to open, right-click/
Command-click and a context menu appears. Choose Open With > Adobe
Fireworks, and the image will be launched within Fireworks (**Figure 14**).

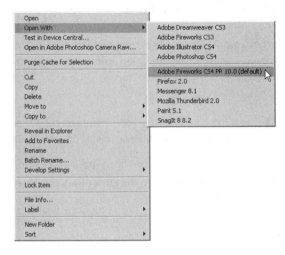

Figure 14 From the context menu you can select which
application opens the file.

#15 Importing Files

Files can be imported into an existing document, saving you the time of opening, copying, and pasting one image into another.

Let's say you are designing a Web interface or building a splash screen for a presentation. You'll want to combine various images into one file for a cohesive design. Importing files into an active document can be a real time-saver.

Select File > Import. Fireworks opens a browsing window that allows you to find the image you want. Click the Open button to return to Fireworks.

Note

Depending on the file type you choose (EPS, AI, or PSD files for example), Fireworks may display a special import dialog—more on this in Technique #17.

The cursor will have changed into an inverted "L" shape. If you simply click on the canvas, the file will be inserted into the currently active layer at its original image size (**Figure 15**).

Figure 15 Importing files can save you a few mouse clicks and gives you the added benefit of being able to scale the image to the correct size in your target document.

However, if you click and drag, you can import the image at a proportionally accurate size suitable for your design. This is more efficient because you do not have to first open the original file, copy it to the new document, and then scale it.

Note

Importing a file does not establish a link to the original file in any way. The imported image is a stand-alone graphic.

#16 Opening Photoshop Files

Fireworks CS4 sports a significant update in Photoshop integration. Opening layered Photoshop files within Fireworks is as simple as choosing File > Open or File > Import and browsing for the native Photoshop PSD file. Fireworks CS4 supports hierarchical Photoshop layers, layer groups, layer styles, layer comps, vector layers, and common blend modes, making it easy to handle files received from another designer.

Exceptions to this integration include adjustment layers and clipping groups. These features are ignored when you import or open a PSD file within Fireworks.

You can customize how Fireworks imports or opens PSD files by using the Photoshop Import category in the Preferences dialog. Select Edit > Preferences on Windows and choose Photoshop Import. On Mac OS X, choose Fireworks > Preferences. Select the Photoshop Import category.

This dialog has been completely overhauled in CS4 (**Figure 16a**).

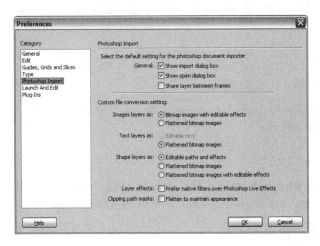

Figure 16a The new Photoshop Import dialog has been greatly improved. You now have more control over the import process.

The General Photoshop Import options include:

- **Show import dialog box/Show open dialog box.** (These are identical dialogs that give you document-level import control). You can override your main preferences: Choose a specific layer comp to open and indicate where to import it to.

- **Share layer between frames.** This option is important for animation or "page state" effects.

The Custom file conversion settings area includes the following options. Images layers as:

- **Bitmap images with editable effects.** This is the default setting that gives you the most flexibility. Layer styles remain editable.

- **Flattened bitmap images.** Flattens layer effects and blend modes to maintain the exact appearance. Photoshop layer styles are no longer editable.

Text layers as:

- **Editable text.** This is the default.

- **Flattened bitmap images.** Preserves the look and style of text, but it is no longer editable.

Shape layers as:

- **Editable paths and effects.** The default option with the most flexibility, but vectors may not render exactly as in Photoshop.

- **Flattened bitmap images.** Vectors and effects are rasterized to bitmaps.

- **Flattened bitmap images with editable effects.** Vectors are rasterized, but layer effects and blend modes remain editable.

Layer effects:

- **Prefer native filters over Photoshop Live Effects.** This option is only recommended if the file will not be going back to Photoshop.

Clipping path masks:

- **Flatten to maintain appearance.** The mask is converted to a bitmap mask.

With the defaults left as they are, opening or importing a PSD file will display the Photoshop File Open Options or File Import Options dialog (**Figure 16b**). They are the same dialog with different titles, and they give you the opportunity to set just-in-time options for opening a PSD, which will override any preferences you may have set in the past.

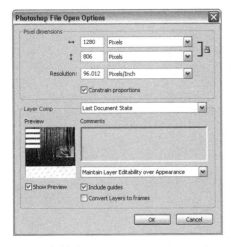

Figure 16b The Photoshop File Open/Import Options dialog gives you a chance to set image dimensions, resolution, and Layer Comp settings.

What Is a Layer Comp?

A layer comp is somewhat similar to pages in Fireworks in that each layer comp can show a different set of visible elements or different positions for those elements. These comps are created in Photoshop by opening the Layer Comps panel and essentially making an editable *snapshot* of the current state of the design.

#17 Opening Adobe Illustrator Files

Opening EPS Files

Fireworks will import EPS files as flattened image files if they were saved in Photoshop. Some EPS files exported from Illustrator may retain their vector information. For most EPS files you are presented with a Vector File Options dialog that allows you some control over the original artwork before it is flattened:

- **Image Size.** Determines the image dimensions and the units in which the image is rendered. You can select from pixels, percent, inches, and centimeters.

- **Resolution.** Indicates the pixels per unit for the resolution.

- **Constrain Proportions.** Maintains the same proportions as the original.

- **Anti-aliased.** Smoothes jagged edges in the opened EPS file.

Because of its vector roots, Fireworks has always had more in common with Illustrator and Freehand than it has with bitmap programs such as Photoshop. Working with vectors in Fireworks is much more akin to Illustrator rather than Photoshop.

Fireworks can open native CS3 and CS4 Illustrator files and preserves hierarchical layers, patterns, linked images, text attributes, transparency, paths, clipping masks, and a great deal more.

When you try to open or import an AI file, a vector import dialog appears (**Figure 17**). Oddly, you do not have direct access to this dialog within the Preferences dialog. It only appears when you open a vector file such as AI or FH (Freehand).

Figure 17 Like the Photoshop File Import Options dialog, the Vector File Options dialog allows you to make changes to the vector file you are importing.

You can set the following options when importing AI, EPS, or FH vector graphics:

- **Scale.** Specifies the scale percentage for the imported file (default is 100%).

- **Width and Height.** Specifies the width and height of the imported file in pixels, inches, or centimeters.

- **Resolution.** Specifies the resolution of the imported file.

- **Anti-alias Paths and Text (selected by default).** Smoothes imported objects to avoid jagged edges. You can choose this option separately for paths or text.

  Note
  Use the Property Inspector to change selected objects to Anti-Alias or Hard Edge.

The File Conversion area specifies how multipage documents are handled when they are imported.

- **Open a page.** Imports only the specified page.

- **Open pages as frames.** Imports all the pages from the document and places each in a separate frame.

- **Ignore layers.** Imports all objects on a single layer.

- **Remember layers.** Maintains the layer structure of the imported file.

- **Convert layers to frames.** Places each layer of the imported document into a separate frame.

- **Include invisible layers.** Imports objects on layers that have been hidden. Otherwise, invisible layers are ignored.

- **Include background layers.** Imports objects from the document's background layer. Otherwise, the background layer is ignored.

- **Render as images.** Rasterizes (flattens) complex groups, blends, or tiled fills and places each as a single bitmap object in a Fireworks document. Enter a number in the text box to determine how many objects a group, blend, or tiled fill can contain before it is rasterized during import.

Save Versus Export— What's the Difference?

In the Fireworks workflow, saving files is generally done if the image is not intended for the Web. For example, the image might be a design comp in progress, a high-resolution JPEG or TIFF file, or be destined for another use other than the Web.

To create Web-ready graphics, the workflow is to optimize the image using the Optimization panel and then Export the file.

The difference between these two options is important.

One consistency between the two is that the exported or saved file is based on the currently visible layers of your design. If the resulting file is a flattened file such as a TIFF, JPEG, GIF, or standard PNG, hidden layers are discarded when exported or saved. Formats such as Fireworks PNG, Photoshop PSD, and to an extent Illustrator AI retain the layer as a hidden layer.

#18 Zen and the Art of Saving Files

Flattening an Image

As you work in Fireworks, you will probably add objects (text, vectors, and other bitmap images). As they are added, these elements become independent objects in the Layers panel with flexibility for editing.

When a multiobject or multilayer file is saved as a standard graphics file such as JPEG or GIF, or standard PNG, Fireworks will merge (flatten) all the objects and layers into a single object on a single layer. Most standard file formats do not support multiple layers or objects like the native formats, such as PSD, AI, and Fireworks PNG.

You can also elect to flatten (merge) objects in the Fireworks document. Select the objects and then choose Modify > Flatten Selection. This is a permanent change. Once the file is closed and reopened, you will not be able to "unflatten" those objects.

You can merge your layers into one by choosing Modify > Flatten Layers. This keeps all your image objects distinct but places them all into one layer. This is not a selective command; every layer you have in the file will be flattened.

When you open a file other than a Fireworks PNG in Fireworks, it is invisibly converted to a Fireworks PNG file, making all the editing tools and features of Fireworks available for use.

If you open a JPEG file just to retouch, crop, or color correct the file without using any of the Fireworks native features such as layers, frames, pages, vectors, or Live Filters, you can simply save the file when you're done by selecting File > Save. You are not prompted to make any optimization settings such as compression/quality (JPEG) or number of colors (GIF or flattened PNG).

Typically, Fireworks designers prefer a more flexible workflow. By employing Fireworks native features, file alterations tend to remain editable at all times, even after opening and closing the file. The examples listed in the previous paragraph follow more of a traditional, permanent (also known as destructive) workflow, common in many bitmap editing programs, especially older ones.

Likewise, if you open a Fireworks PNG file and make changes to it, saving the file does not activate any other prompts. You can save the following file formats directly: Fireworks PNG, GIF, animated GIF, JPEG, BMP, WBMP, TIFF, SWF, AI, PSD, and PICT (Mac only). By directly I mean if you open a GIF file you can simply press Ctrl/Command + S to save the file with the same name and format.

If you want to save your file in a format other than the original, selecting File > Save As offers you a list of formats to choose from as well as a button to alter format-specific options such as quality settings and image size for the desired format (**Figure 18**). These options can also be set in the Image Preview dialog (File > Image Preview).

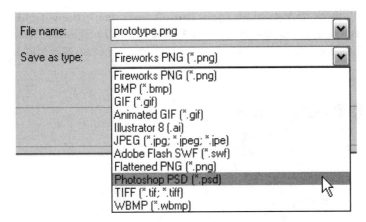

Figure 18 The Save as type drop-down menu gives you a variety of formats in which to save your image.

If you have used the enhanced features of Fireworks on a standard file format, when you try to save the file, you will be prompted to save it as a Fireworks PNG to maintain its editability.

Saving files will also maintain any metadata (such as camera details or copyright info) that exists in the file. Exporting files strips this information from the files to further reduce the file size.

Exporting Your Goods

Exporting your images is a fundamental part of the Fireworks workflow, which consists of optimizing, previewing, and then exporting images.

If graphics are destined for the Web (or screen), the next step after editing is to optimize the file.

The Optimize panel is a key component in this process. You set the file format and quality settings in this panel. The Preview tabs (Preview, 2-Up, and 4-Up) show you how your file will look based on the optimization settings you set. The 2-Up and 4-UP tabs display multiple windows, where you can experiment further with the optimize settings and make visual comparisons between JPEG and GIF images, for example.

#19 Exporting a Single File

Select the file format you would like to use for exporting in the Optimize panel and set format-specific options (**Figure 19**). Web images should be JPEG, GIF, or PNG. JPEG, PNG 24, or PNG 32 is best for photos; GIF or PNG-8 is best for line art or illustrations.

Exporting Files with the Export Wizard

If you're new to exporting images for Web use, the Export Wizard can help you with your decisions. The wizard asks you questions about the intended use of the image and offers suggestions for file format and ways to reduce the file size of the image.

You can also ask the wizard to target a specific file size.

To use the wizard, select File > Export Wizard and follow the prompts.

Figure 19 In the Optimize panel, you can choose from a series of preset format options or customize the format and compression settings to your liking.

1. Choose File > Export.

2. Select a location to export the image file to. If the graphic is for a specific Web site, the best spot for it is usually in a folder within your local Web site folder.

3. Enter a filename. Fireworks sets the file extension based on your optimization settings.

4. Select Images Only from the Export drop-down menu.

5. Click Save.

To export your image in smaller pieces, you must first slice your document and then export only slices. For more on slicing, see Chapter 5, "Working with Multiple Images."

#20 Using the Image Preview Dialog

The Image Preview dialog (File > Image Preview; **Figure 20**) is similar to the Preview, 2-Up, and 4-Up tabs found in the main document window. It combines a preview as well as optimization inputs for setting pixel dimensions, file format, compression, and even cropping. This window is quite handy if you need to occasionally output your image or design in a manner different from your usual workflow. For example, you might normally export a final graphic as a JPEG, but someone may have specifically requested a TIFF file. Or you may have a fully fleshed-out design but want to send a highly compressed file or a file that is smaller in size (for use as a thumbnail image).

Figure 20 The Image Preview dialog gives you another way to export a file in a different format or file size.

This window gives you the same control over exporting the image as you'll find in the Optimize panel.

#21 Using the Export Area Tool

The Export Area tool is one of those hidden gems in the Fireworks treasure box (**Figure 21a**). Found beneath the Crop tool, the Export Area tool lets you draw a crop around a specific area of your design and then export a flattened version of that area. Like all the export functions, the resulting file is based on what is currently visible in the Layers panel.

Figure 21a Export area is similar to cropping an image, but you are sent directly to the Image Preview dialog when you approve the crop dimensions.

Select the tool and drag across the document to designate an area for export. While you're in drawing mode, you can adjust the position of the marquee. Press and hold the spacebar to drag the marquee to another location on the canvas. Release the spacebar to continue drawing the marquee. Releasing the mouse button leaves the export area marquee selected.

Once you've set the area, you can resize it if necessary (**Figure 21b**).

- Shift-drag a handle to resize the marquee proportionally.

- Alt-drag (Windows) or Option-drag (Mac) a handle to resize the marquee from the center.

- Alt-Shift-drag (Windows) or Option-Shift-drag (Mac) a handle to constrain the proportions and resize the marquee from the center.

- Double-click or right-click within the export area to launch the Image Preview dialog. Make any changes necessary to the format, compression, or dimensions, and then click Export.

Figure 21b Using the Export Area tool to crop a small area of an image.

#22 Creating PDF files

Hands up those of you who have experienced the pain and anguish of printing files from Fireworks. As mentioned in Chapter 1, "Getting Started," Fireworks is a screen graphics app. It does not excel at printing designs or graphics and is not optimized to do so.

Enter Adobe PDF. Creating a PDF of a design concept is just another way to deliver the goods to your client. The advantage of PDF is that you can easily print a design or it can be viewed onscreen. In either case, the end user does not need a lot of technical experience to view the file.

In CS4 you finally have some relief from printing angst in the form of a PDF Export feature. Simply select File > Export and choose Adobe PDF from the Export drop-down menu.

If you want further control or to password protect the PDF file, click the Options button in the main Export dialog and the Adobe PDF Export Options dialog will open (**Figure 22**).

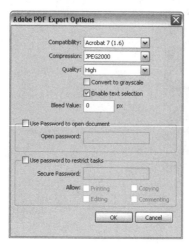

Figure 22 The Adobe PDF Export Options dialog gives you additional control over the file to be created.

If you or your client requires hard copy output of a design, exporting as a PDF file is the way to go. Adobe Reader is a ubiquitous plug-in, and Acrobat has far better control over printing than Fireworks. The right tool for the right job, as they say.

Note

Printing resolution issues still apply. If you create your design at screen resolution (default resolution for Fireworks is 96 ppi) rather than print resolution (usually around 300 ppi), the image quality of the final output will be mediocre at best.

Making Interactive PDFs

The PDF export feature has more uses than basic printing. As your designs progress, you might start building clickable graphic prototypes of site designs. One way to send your client these prototypes would be in the form of an interactive PDF file.

PDF export supports hyperlinks created with Fireworks in the form of hotspots and slices. These hyperlinks can be to another page within the PNG design or to an external Web site. Creating slices is covered in Chapter 6, "The Big Picture on Web Graphics" and creating and exporting prototypes is covered in more detail in Chapter 12, "Designing Interfaces."

#23 Saving Photoshop Files

Adobe is big on integrating its stable of products. This was evident even before programs like Fireworks, Dreamweaver, and Flash were part of the equation. With each product cycle, Fireworks and Photoshop come closer to a fully integrated working relationship.

Text, hierarchical layers, layer groups, vector shapes, fills (solid color only), and masked objects are maintained and supported when you save a file in PSD format from within Fireworks.

If your designs and comps must go from Fireworks to Photoshop for alteration, and you want to retain as much editability as possible, make sure you save a copy of your file in the Photoshop PSD format. Select File > Save As, and then choose Photoshop PSD from the Save as type drop-down menu (**Figure 23**): Save as type will change to Save copy as when you choose Photoshop PSD.

Figure 23 Always save a version of your file as a Photoshop file if it will require editing in Photoshop at a later date. Opening a Fireworks PNG file in Photoshop will flatten *all* the layers and effects.

When in Fireworks, you can gain additional integration by only applying Live Filters or blend modes, which are common to both Fireworks and Photoshop. See the sidebars "Common Blend Modes Supported by Photoshop and Fireworks" and "Common Live Filters."

Note

If a Fireworks PNG file is opened in another application, such as Photoshop, the file is flattened. If you save the file within another graphics application, all the editable benefits of a Fireworks PNG file are lost.

Common Live Filters

Photoshop Live Filters can be added while in Fireworks, or they can be supported (editable) or maintained (only editable in Photoshop) if they are added as a layer style in Photoshop.

The following list of Live Filters are supported and maintained between Photoshop and Fireworks:

- Drop Shadow, Inner Shadow
- Glow, Inner Glow
- Bevel and Emboss (all)

Common Blend Modes For Photoshop and Fireworks

Normal

Dissolve

Darken

Multiply

Color Burn

Linear Burn

Lighten

Screen

Color Dodge

Linear Dodge

Overlay

Soft Light

Hard Light

Vivid Light

Linear Light

Pin Light

Hard Mix

Difference

Exclusion

Hue

Saturation

Color

Luminosity

CHAPTER THREE

Working with Bitmap Images

Graphics play a big role in Web design and creation. Fireworks gives you an excellent basic, but effective set of bitmap tools to create, edit, and correct bitmap images. This chapter focuses on the core skills of correction and manipulation of bitmaps. More creative techniques can be found in Chapter 8, "Exploring Creative Options."

In many cases, the photographs you work with are supplied by a client. They may be professionally shot images, or they may be images created by the client. Being able to improve the quality of an image when necessary is essential, and Fireworks brings to the table a core set of editing tools. Pretty much *any* image taken directly from a digital camera or a scanner can benefit from some basic tonal and color corrections.

Before going any further, here's a little info on bitmap and vector images. Fireworks can work easily with both bitmap images and vector artwork on the same canvas, so it's best to understand their differences.

A bitmap image (also referred to as raster image) is made up of a set number of pixels, for example, 300 pixels wide by 200 pixels high. This pixel count is the *image resolution*. Each pixel has its own physical location, color, and brightness. If you enlarge or reduce (resample) a bitmap image, you change the number of pixels that make up the image, which usually tends to reduce image quality.

A vector image is a mathematical description of a shape or path and as a result can be resized with no obvious damage to the object. While vector images are not made up of pixels, they can contain a bitmap fill such as a pattern, texture, or color. These bitmap elements can be affected when a vector is resized.

#24 Resizing Images

In many situations you may receive image files from a client that are far too large for use in a Web page. A fairly large image on a Web page is considered to be no more than 500–600 pixels at its longest dimension. Note that this refers to inline content, which is part of the page content, not special images such as header or footer images or (sometimes) background images.

Resizing images is a snap in Fireworks. Open the file and select Modify > Canvas > Image Size (Ctrl/Command+J). As discussed earlier, the pixel dimensions are the important measurements for a Web image. Make sure Constrain Proportions is selected (unless you want to distort the image), and type in a new value for either the height or the width. The other field will update with the new relative size. Click OK.

To avoid accidentally overwriting an image, you can also open files in Fireworks as *untitled*. When you attempt to save the file, Fireworks prompts you for a new filename.

Tip
If you need to resize supplied or purchased images, be sure to keep the original versions safe in case they are needed later. I usually create a folder to hold all the original art for a client. As I modify images, I save them to a production folder in a suitable format. My preference is to save files as Fireworks PNG files because the format is nonlossy. If I resave my file as a JPEG, for example, compression (and quality loss) will be applied each time.

#25 Improving Images with Levels Filters

Your images can come from a variety of sources: a client, your own camera or scanner, or stock image agencies. If the image you receive is too bright or too dark, using a filter can improve the overall image quality in a permanent or editable manner as noted in the "Where Are the Filters?" sidebar.

When using filters from the Filters menu, create a copy of your image by dragging the object to the New Bitmap Image icon at the bottom of the Layers panel, as shown in **Figure 25a**. So if you really make a mess of the image (hey, it happens), your original image will be protected.

Figure 25a Create a copy of your image so the original is not damaged.

Live Filters, however, give you much more flexibility because the filter remains editable at all times, even after the file has been saved as a Fireworks PNG file, closed, and reopened.

Where Are the Filters?

The core Fireworks' filters can be found in three locations: the Filters menu in the main menu bar, the Live Filters menu in the Property Inspector, and the Image Editing panel.

The Filters menu and the Image Editing panel produce permanent pixel changes; once the file is saved and closed, you can't undo the effect. The filters can be applied to bitmap images or bitmap image selections.

The Live Filters menu in the Property Inspector offers the same filters and more, and they always remain editable. You can apply Live Filters to an entire bitmap object, as well as vector objects, but you cannot use Live Filters on a bitmap selection.

You can also download many third-party filters, which will work in Fireworks.

What's a Histogram?

A histogram is a visual representation of pixel brightness distribution in your image. How's that for a geeky explanation? The histogram shows you a range of shadows (left) to highlights (right). The midtone pixels are in the center. The horizontal axis represents color values from darkest (0) to brightest (255).

The vertical axis represents the number of pixels at each brightness level. Typically, you should adjust the highlights and shadows first; as you do, the midtone slider will move. Adjusting the midtone slider after adjusting the highlights and shadows lets you improve the brightness of the midtone values without affecting the highlights and shadows. Midtones are the values that represent the middle range of brightness in an image. These tones are not excessively bright or dark.

Click on the image in either the Layers panel or the canvas. Click the Add Filters button in the Property Inspector **(Figure 25b)** to expand the Live Filters menu. Choose Adjust Color > Levels.

Figure 25b Live filters remain editable at all times.

Beneath the histogram chart are three sliders: black, gray, and white **(Figure 25c)**. You can drag these sliders to darken, lighten, or reduce the contrast of an image. Dragging the black slider to the right darkens the image, in essence setting a new "black point"—the darkest part of an image. Dragging the white slider to the left brightens the image. The midtone (gray) slider should be adjusted after you've made your major adjustments with the black and white sliders.

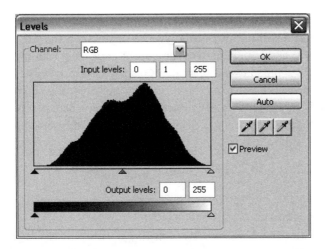

Figure 25c Adjusting the three sliders under the histogram can improve color saturation and tonal range.

If you see gaps on the left or right of the histogram chart or if there is very little of the histogram visible on either side, it may mean the image is too dark or too light. Just drag the black and white sliders until they line up with the edges of the chart, and you should see a noticeable improvement to the quality of your image.

How Dark/Light Is Too Dark/Light?

Mac and Windows computers have different display gammas, which means your images will look a bit different on the opposing platform. Fireworks has a nifty feature to help you gauge the brightness of your image on the *other* platform. From the View menu choose either PC or Macintosh Gamma. You'll only see the option for the platform you are not using.

#26 Using Selection Tools to Alter Specific Areas

Repeat after me, "To have an effect, you must select."

Making selections on a bitmap image gives you control over the pixels in a specific area and is an important component of working with bitmaps regardless of the software application. Creating a selection isolates the work you do to one area of an image, protecting all other areas from being altered. For example, you might want to brighten a dark part of an image. Without a selection, this change in pixel brightness would be applied to the entire photo.

Object Selection Versus Bitmap Selection

Clicking on an object (bitmap, vector, text) within the canvas or in the Layers panel selects (or make active) that particular object in its entirety. You can then move, delete, or alter the entire object. When an object is selected, a light blue border surrounds the object. You can change this highlight color in the Preferences dialog, General category.

Object selections are different from bitmap selections; a bitmap selection actually selects the pixels within a bitmap image. You make bitmap selections so you can apply changes to a portion of a bitmap image rather than to the entire image. A bitmap selection is identified by a characteristic marquee, which is referred to as *marching ants*. You can't apply a bitmap selection to a vector object or to text. It can only be applied to an object made up of pixels, like a digital photo.

If you want to select a vector using the bitmap tools, you must first convert (rasterize) it to a bitmap by choosing Modify > Flatten Selection or Modify > Convert Path to Marquee. Once converted to a bitmap, the object (shape or text) loses all vector features, so you might want to first make a duplicate of the object in its vector format.

Fireworks' selection tools include the Marquee and Oval Marquee, Lasso and Polygon Lasso, and the Magic Wand (**Figure 26a**).

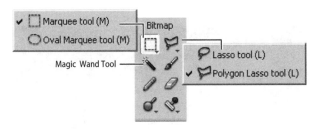

Figure 26a Many similar tools in the Tools panel are grouped. Click and hold on the small triangle in the lower-right corner of a tool to access more tools in that group.

The selection tools are very helpful if you want to alter or copy a specific area of an image. Choose the selection tool most suitable for the job. Use the Rectangular or Elliptical Marquee tool to select regularly shaped areas. One of the Lasso tools may be better suited to select irregular areas when you make a selection freehand. If the area is full of similar colors, the Magic Wand may be your best choice to quickly create a selection.

The Magic Wand selects pixels based on color. If you have an area of similarly colored pixels in your image (a blue sky, for example), the Magic Wand can quickly select that part of your image. Start the selection by clicking the Magic Wand tool on an area of your image. The Magic Wand selects contiguous pixels of the same color range (Tolerance setting). You can increase the tool's sensitivity by changing the Tolerance setting in the Property Inspector to a higher value.

As with the other bitmap selection tools, the selection edge can be set to Hard, Anti-Alias, or Feather. A Hard edge produces a jagged pixilated selection. Anti-Alias blends the selection with the area outside the selection, and Feather creates a much less accurate, soft, blended edge selection. Unlike the other two edge settings, you can apply a pixel value to Feather to increase the blend between the inside and outside of the selection.

Note
When applying a filter adjustment to a selection, you must use the main Filters menu. You should also create a copy of the image before you begin.

Using Live Marquee

The Live Marquee feature is available for all bitmap selection tools. By default, it is active (selected) in the Property Inspector. Live Marquee gives you immediate control over the edge of your bitmap selection. You can choose Hard for an aliased hard-edged selection; Anti-Alias for a softer, slightly blended selection edge; or Feather for a very soft blend. When you choose Feather, you can set the amount of feathering you want. This amount gradually blends any effect applied to the bitmap selection on both the inner and outer edges of the selection.

I used the Live Marquee feature in the Property Inspector to set the selection edge to Anti-Alias in Figure 26b.

In **Figure 26b**, I used the Polygon Lasso to select the window area, which was too bright, and then selected Filter > Adjust Color > Levels to enhance the area.

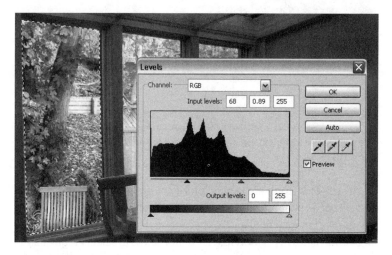

Figure 26b The Polygon Lasso tool makes selecting irregularly shaped areas effortless.

Tip
It's a good idea to zoom in on the area you are selecting to ensure a more accurate selection.

If you must create a particularly complex selection, you might want to save your efforts as an Alpha Channel. Choose Select > Save Bitmap Selection **(Figure 26c)**. You can name the selection, and then call it up any time you need it during your session. If you save the file as a Fireworks PNG file, the selection will remain with the file.

Figure 26c Saving complex selections can save you time later on if you need that selection again.

Additional Selection Features for the Marquee

If you choose the Rectangular or Elliptical Marquee, the Property Inspector offers you additional options:

- **Normal.** Creates a marquee in which the height and width are independent of each other.

- **Fixed Ratio.** Constrains the height and width to defined ratios.

- **Fixed Size.** Sets the height and width to a defined dimension, in pixels.

Showing or Hiding a Bitmap Selection

Sometimes the marquee can get in your way. You can quickly show or hide the *marching ants* by pressing Ctrl/Command+H.

#27 Retouching with the Rubber Stamp Tool

The Rubber Stamp tool has been around since the early days of digital imaging. It's used to remove unwanted objects by "painting" over them with a sample from another part of the image.

Using it requires a two-step process: You first sample an undamaged area by Alt/Option-clicking. You then paint over the damaged area to remove artifacts or unwanted details. The Rubber Stamp makes an exact copy of pixels from elsewhere in the image, so when you're choosing a sampling area, make sure the area is similar in color and brightness to the area you want to fix.

Because the stamp permanently affects pixels, it's a good idea to work on a duplicate of your image, an empty bitmap image, or a new layer so your original image won't be affected

You can create a duplicate of your image by dragging the image from the Layers panel to the New Bitmap Image icon at the bottom of the panel.

You can create an empty bitmap image by clicking on the New Bitmap Image icon, or create a new layer by clicking the New Layer icon. Both icons are found at the bottom of the Layers panel.

To ensure the empty image or layer appears in the right place, make sure your original image is selected in the Layers panel first, and then add your empty bitmap image or new layer (**Figure 27a**). This creates a new

Figure 27a You can use a new bitmap image or empty layer to add your Rubber Stamp corrections.

(transparent) bitmap image or a new layer directly above the currently selected image. If you take this route, be sure to select the "Use entire document" check box in the Property Inspector, so the Rubber Stamp tool will sample your original image pixels **(Figure 27b)**. By default, the stamp only samples from the currently active layer or image.

If you want to reduce the appearance of wrinkles in a face or in fabric without eliminating them completely, set the Opacity of the Rubber Stamp tool to a low value, such as 80%.

Figure 27b The Property Inspector controls attributes for many of the tools in the Tools panel.

Localized Editing

The Blur, Sharpen, Dodge, Burn, and Smudge tools are part of the same tool set in the Tools panel. Each tool lets you selectively change an image using a brush. Tool properties are controlled using the Property Inspector.

Blur and Sharpen tools share the same attributes: brush size, edge softness, pixel shape, and intensity.

Dodge and Burn tools derive their names from photo darkroom techniques. Dodging an image area brightens the area. Burning an area darkens it. These tools introduce two other controls: range and exposure. Range lets you choose the brightness range you want to alter: highlights, midtones, or shadows. Exposure is similar to the Blur tool's Intensity setting. The higher the value, the more obvious the effect.

The Smudge tool is like finger painting with pixels. You literally push pixels around the canvas. Along with the standard brush controls, you will find a Pressure setting and a Smudge color check box. Pressure affects the intensity of the smudge, and if you activate the smudge color, you can choose a color to add to the color mix.

Remember that these tools permanently change the pixels in your image.

Modifier Keys for Bitmap Tools

The Shift and Alt/Option keys add some handy functionality. With all the tools, the Shift key constrains your work to a perfectly straight line. Holding down the Alt/Option key toggles the effect for each tool: The Sharpen tool switches to the Blur tool and vice versa; the Dodge tool switches temporarily to the Burn tool. Release the key and the tool returns to its original state.

With the Smudge tool, holding down Alt/Option activates the current smudge color.

Use these tools at low intensities for a subtle effect. You can always build on the effect by painting over the area again.

#28 Masking One Image with Another

You can use the tonal range of one image to mask another. Using a bitmap image (a photo, for example) as a mask converts the image to grayscale. Bright areas in the mask show the image being masked; dark areas hide the masked object. Any parts of the mask that are gray will be semitransparent. You can create some interesting and unique background graphic treatments in this manner (**Figure 28a**).

Figure 28a This metal image is masked by a photo of some ferns. In the dark areas of the ferns, you can see a gradient object showing through.

To use a bitmap as a mask, make sure the image is above the photo you want to mask in the Layers panel. Select both photos, and then select Modify > Mask > Group as Mask. The mask appears as a thumbnail beside the image being masked **(Figure 28b)**.

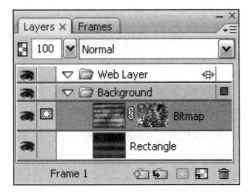

Figure 28b Any image that is converted to a mask changes to a grayscale appearance, because transparency is based on grayscale values.

When you use a bitmap image as a mask, you can also use filters to further adjust the effect of the mask.

#29 Creating a Bitmap Mask with a Selection

Using a selection to create a mask is a quick and easy way to get creative. The great advantage of masking is that it is nondestructive and flexible; you can hide parts of an image without permanently deleting them. Using the Brush, you can easily edit the mask live on the canvas.

Use any of the bitmap selection tools to create your selection. Decide on the type of edge you want for the selection (Hard, Anti-Alias, Feather) using the Live Marquee settings in the Property Inspector.

Click the Add Mask icon in the Layers panel (**Figure 29a**). A mask icon appears beside the image being masked. This type of mask is also referred to as a bitmap mask.

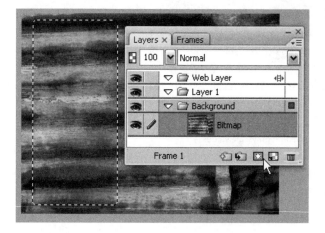

Figure 29a Adding a mask is as easy as clicking the Add Mask icon in the Layers panel.

You're done! The mask is created from the selection and hides anything that appears outside the marquee (**Figure 29b**).

Sidebar Communications

Lorem ipsum dolor sit amet, consectetuer adipiscing elit, sed diam nonummy nibh euismod tincidunt ut laoreet dolore magna aliquam erat volutpat. Ut wisi enim ad minim veniam, quis nostrud exerci tation ullamcorper suscipit lobortis nisl ut aliquip ex ea commodo consequat. Duis autem vel eum iriure dolor in hendrerit in vulputate velit esse molestie consequat, vel illum dolore eu feugiat nulla facilisis at vero eros et accumsan et iusto odio dignissim qui blandit praesent luptatum zzril delenit augue duis dolore te feugait nulla facilisi.

Lorem ipsum dolor sit amet, consectetuer adipiscing elit, sed diam nonummy nibh euismod tincidunt ut laoreet dolore magna aliquam erat volutpat. Ut wisi enim ad minim veniam, quis nostrud exerci tation ullamcorper suscipit lobortis nisl ut aliquip ex ea commodo consequat. Duis autem vel eum iriure dolor in hendrerit in vulputate velit esse molestie consequat, vel illum dolore eu feugiat nulla facilisis at vero eros et accumsan et iusto odio dignissim qui blandit praesent luptatum zzril delenit augue duis dolore te feugait nulla facilisi.

Figure 29b The metal photo has been masked using a feathered selection.

Quick Background Removal

You can remove a background from an image in several ways.

- Permanently remove the background by using the Eraser tool, painting over the unwanted background to delete it.

- Select the background using the Lasso, Polygon Lasso, or Magic Wand and press Delete.

- Use a mask for ultimate flexibility, because you never truly delete the pixels. Let's say you have a product photo shot on a plain background, but you want to jazz things up a bit.

  1. Select the background using the bitmap selection tool of your choice. If the background is even toned, the Magic Wand is probably a good choice.

  2. Once the selection is complete, choose Select > Select Inverse to change the selection from the background to the product.

  3. Click the Add Mask icon located at the bottom of the Layers panel to create a bitmap mask. You can then import a new image to act as the background for the product shot.

  4. Adjust the mask further by using the Brush tool, in case your original bitmap selection was not as refined as you wanted.

Select Inverse— Other Uses

Select Inverse is used to toggle the active selection between the original selection and the nonselected areas. Sometimes, selecting the unwanted part of an image is easiest.

Let's say you have a photo of a cityscape with a clear sky in the background, and you want to do some levels or filter adjustments to the cityscape. It's easier (and faster) to use the Magic Wand tool to select the even-colored sky rather than to select the cityscape. Then choose Select > Select Inverse to reverse the selected areas, making the cityscape the active selection.

Select Similar

Choose Select > Select Similar to add to the current bitmap selection based on colors within the active selection. Anywhere the colors within the selection appear throughout the image will become part of the new selection. Use this command with any bitmap selection.

Modifying a Selection

You can expand, contract, or smooth an active bitmap selection by choosing the Select menu, and then choosing the desired action.

Well, it can be that easy. But chances are you might want to tweak that mask, which is also easy to do.

Select the mask icon in the Layers panel. Choose the Brush tool. The Brush tool uses the Stroke color box for its color selection. You can choose the color (black, white, or a shade of gray for masks) from either the Property Inspector or the Stroke color box in the Tools panel.

Black adds to the mask (hiding the image), white subtracts from the mask (showing more of the image), and shades of gray results in a semitransparent effect.

All the attributes of the Brush tool are at your disposal. You can change the size, edge softness, and texture, or even choose a custom stroke effect from the Stroke drop-down menu. In **Figure 29c** I used black with a soft brush to hide more of the image, creating a wavy style.

Figure 29c Use the Brush tool to edit a bitmap mask. Just paint over the mask area you want to change.

If the mask is not what you want, just drag it to the trash icon in the Layers panel. Fireworks prompts you to discard or apply the mask when it is deleted.

CHAPTER FOUR

Staying on the (Vector) Path

Computer drawing tools use mathematical equations to draw lines and fills on the screen are known as *vectors*. A vector is simply the path between two defined points on the screen with properties applied to them, such as color and thickness. By combining paths and points, a computer can draw almost any shape using vector tools like those found in Fireworks and other vector-based applications such as Adobe Illustrator.

#30 Using Vector Tools

Fireworks has always had a decent and easy to use set of vector tools. Most of them are found in the Tools panel in their own section. A whole series of prebuilt Auto Shapes are also found in the Shapes panel (more on those later) shown in **Figure 30a**.

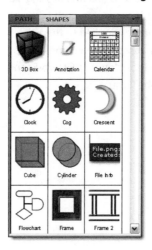

Figure 30a You will find many more shapes in the Shapes panel.

Using vectors is pretty intuitive in Fireworks, but to the new user, they may seem a bit intimidating. Just so you know, I cut my teeth on vectors using Fireworks. They're nothing like bitmap images or bitmap tools. With a bit of practice you'll be creating your own custom vector shapes and masks before you know it (**Figure 30b**).

Figure 30b Several vector tools have additional tools that appear when you press and hold the mouse button over the main tool icon.

#31 Using Shapes as Image Elements

Bitmap images are a huge part of Web site design, but vectors come in very handy for many tasks as well, from masking a bitmap object to creating a container (often referred to as a "pod" these days to hold page elements) to creating the look of UI components for an application design.

The visual components of vectors consist of a *Fill* and a *Stroke*. You can use both or just one on any vector, depending on the use of the vector. In fact, if you take a close look at the Tools panel (**Figure 31a**), you will see that your color options refer to Fill (paint bucket) and Stroke (pencil).

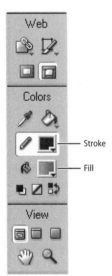

Figure 31a Fireworks sets colors just like other vector applications do. It uses Stroke and Fill rather than foreground and background colors as you would find in a bitmap application like Photoshop.

The Fireworks' Property Inspector lets you use Fill Categories other than just solid color for a vector shape. You can *fill* a path with a pattern, texture, gradient, or solid color (**Figure 31b**).

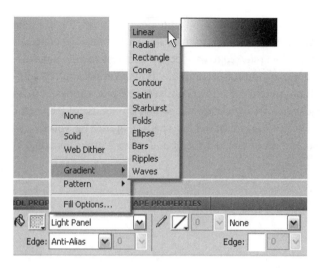

Figure 31b You can fill a vector shape with a variety of choices—all from the Property Inspector.

You can also use several preset Stroke settings, all of which are customizable via the Stroke Options item in the Stroke menu (**Figure 31c**).

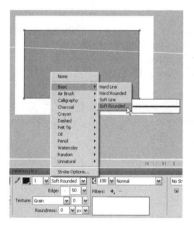

Figure 31c You can use one of many preset stroke styles or create your own.

1. Select the Rectangle tool in the Tools panel and draw a shape on the canvas.

   If you have Tooltips active, you'll see pixel-precise dimensions of the shape as you draw it.

2. Let go of the shape and the current Fill and Stroke will be applied.

   Note
   Fireworks remembers the last settings used in Stroke and Fill. So if you want to use something different, you can change the settings before you draw the shape, or change them afterward by going to the Property Inspector.

3. Set the Fill to a solid color of your liking, but make it a light color.

4. Set the Stroke to black, 1-Pixel Soft Rounded.

5. Use the Property Inspector to add some character by altering the roundness of the corners. You can now set rectangle roundness in either percentages (à la Fireworks CS3 and earlier) or pixels. Using pixels means the corners will not distort when you scale the shape. Set the value to 20 pixels.

   You now have a nice little container for text or the starting point for an interface element for an Adobe AIR application.

6. Select Commands > Text > Lorem Ipsum to take things a bit further. This generates a paragraph of text using the currently chosen font in the Property Inspector.

7. Set the font to Verdana from the Font Family drop-down menu and set the size to 11 pixels (**Figure 31d**).

8. Use the Pointer tool to drag the text object above the container.

9. Use the Pointer tool to click on a blue corner point for the text object and reset the size so the text better fits your container.

Filling Shapes with Patterns, Gradients, and Filters

Create a new document by selecting File > New (Ctrl/Command+N). Choose the Star Shape from the Vector tools and draw it out on the canvas. Change the Fill to a Gradient (I chose the starburst gradient). The shape is filled with the gradient, and control arms appear to control the shape and direction of the gradient. As you drag these control arms, the gradient updates live, so you can judge your results quickly.

Patterns work much the same way. Click the Fill Category drop-down menu and this time select Patterns. These are bitmap images that have been designed to seamlessly tile inside a vector shape. Choose one and you will again see those control arms, which allow you to change the direction of the pattern and even distort it.

Still within the Property Inspector, click the Filters menu and add a Glow (Filters > Shadow and Glow > Glow).

Auto Shapes

The Shapes tools and the Shapes panel also contain objects called Auto Shapes. These shapes (star, arrow, measure tool, spiral, arrow line, etc.) are controlled by JavaScript. You will recognize an Auto Shape by the little yellow diamonds that appear around the object when it is created. If you mouse over these diamonds, you will see that each controls different attributes of the shape. For example, the controls for the Star Auto Shape control the number of points, inner and outer radius, and inner and outer roundness.

Figure 31d Choosing a font family is now separate from choosing a font style (such as bold or italic).

Not bad, eh? Quick and easy! This rounded corner container can also be exported by Fireworks as a CSS layout with an expandable container and true HTML text, but you'll learn more about that in Chapter 13, "Fitting Fireworks into the Design Workflow."

You can use a variety of shapes to create containers, a patterned box for a header, or even your own custom icons and bullets.

#32 Understanding the Transform Tools

Once you've drawn a shape, chances are you'll want to change its size or shape. You can do this in a basic manner by using the Transform tools in the Tools panel. The Transform tools consist of Scale, Skew, Distort, and the new 9-Slice Scaling tool (**Figure 32**). The Transform tools work just as easily on bitmap images.

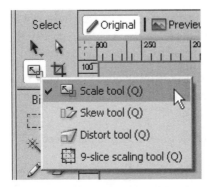

Figure 32 Added to the Transform tool set is the 9-Slice Scaling Transform tool.

> **Note**
> *Keep in mind that scaling a bitmap image larger than its initial size will reduce the image quality. Scaling a vector shape larger than its initial size has no impact on the shape's quality, but if that shape is filled with a pattern or texture (which are bitmaps), make sure you have deselected the Scale Strokes and Effects preference found in the General category of the Preferences panel. This will force the pattern to tile and retain its quality rather than resize and become pixilated.*

For more custom changes to paths, you'll want to work with the Pen tool and the Subselection tool (see Techniques #36 and #37).

#33 Using the Transform Tools

The Scale tool enlarges or reduces a selected object (proportionately, if dragged from a corner).

The Skew tool acts like a perspective tool if you drag the object (bitmap or vector) from a corner, or it skews the image if you drag from a center control handle. In both cases, two control points are affected at the same time.

The Distort tool only drags one corner at a time. You can have a lot of fun with this tool, as evidenced in **Figure 33a**. Using Distort, you can create a forced perspective not only on a vector shape, but also on type!

1. Select a shape (the rectangle shape from Technique #31 is a fine image to work with) and choose the Distort tool (press Q on the keyboard to toggle through the Transform tools).

   Notice the black bounding box that appears around the object.

2. Drag from a corner to pull the shape's corner with the cursor.

3. Drag the bottom-right corner down and the bottom-left corner upward to get a shape similar to the figure shown.

4. Double-click to commit the changes.

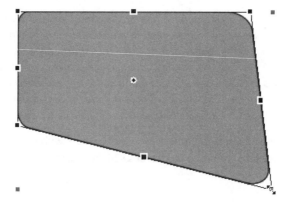

Figure 33a The Distort tool can create exaggerated perspective in a vector or a bitmap.

5. Select a fairly bold font and type a word.

6. Adjust the font size as desired, and then go back to the Distort tool.

7. Drag the bottom-right corner down as you did with the shape. You may want to drag the bottom-left corner up a bit to force the perspective even more.

Despite the distortion, the text remains editable (**Figure 33b**).

Figure 33b Text can also be distorted and remain editable.

Note
The Skew and Distort tools also come in handy if you are trying to correct perspective in a photograph.

#34 Distortion-free Scaling with the 9-Slice Scaling Tool

The 9-Slice Scaling tool provides you with a way to quickly scale an object (vectors usually, but not always) and keep certain areas (such as corners) from becoming distorted as the object is resized. In CS3 you could only apply 9-slice scaling to symbols. But there are many situations in which you might have a particular shape or bitmap used only once in a design. In that case, there's not much point to turning it into a symbol; hence, the 9-Slice Scaling tool.

With pixel-based corner roundness, a standard rectangle scales well when dragged from a corner but not well if the height or width is adjusted independently. More complex shapes, such as a UI panel or navigation panel for a Web site, would have the same distortion difficulties if they were adjusted independently. The example in **Figure 34a** shows an object that could be used in a variety of situations.

Figure 34a A custom path created in Fireworks.

Let's say you decide to widen the object to fill a larger space. Without 9-Slice Scaling, you'd get the result shown in **Figure 34b**.

Figure 34b Scaling a shape in just one direction can produce undesirable results.

By using the 9-Slice Scaling tool and setting the guides to preserve the corners of the shape, you'll get much better results, as shown in **Figure 34c**.

Figure 34c The 9-Slice Scaling tool makes it easy to do *off-the-cuff* scaling without distorting the corners.

The secret to 9-slice scaling, whether it's a symbol, an object, a bitmap, or a vector, is to find safe areas where scaling will not produce any noticeable deformation (**Figure 34d**). With a vector containing a solid fill, that's pretty easy. With more complex shapes, you need to plan out your guides a little more carefully. Photographs are not good candidates for 9-slice scaling, but a screen grab of a software panel might scale quite well using the 9-Slice Scaling tool.

Figure 34d The 9-Slice Scaling guides (dashed lines) reset automatically each time you commit to a scaled size.

Avoid Distortion with a Bitmap Pattern

The example in Technique #34 includes a pattern fill. Even though it is a bitmap pattern, it did not distort because I deselected the Scale Strokes and Effects preference in the General category of the Preferences panel.

#35 Creating a Custom Shape

You might be wondering how I created that L-Shape panel. No? Well, humor me, it's my first book. There is an L-Shape Auto Shape, but except for the upper-left corner, it lacks control for corner roundness.

The shape in Technique #34 was made using two standard rectangles, each with the same corner radius.

1. Draw one corner. Set the rectangle roundness.

2. Duplicate the shape by pressing Ctrl/Command+Shift+D.

3. Using the Pointer tool, move the duplicated shape so that it only covers the area you want to remove from the rectangle.

4. Select both shapes.

5. Open the Path panel.

6. Choose Punch Paths to delete the duplicate shape and the section of the other shape it overlapped (**Figure 35a**). You now have a nice inner corner, but the two outer corners are sharp. Converting them to rounded corners use to be a real pain, but not anymore.

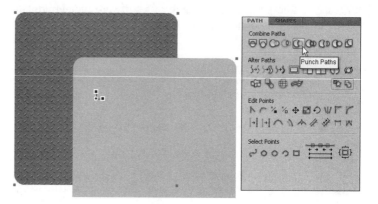

Figure 35a Two vectors must be selected to use the Punch command.

7. Click the Subselection tool and use it to select either of the two sharp corner anchor points.

8. Go to the Path panel again and choose Fillet Points (**Figure 35b**). A dialog prompts you for a corner radius. Set the same value as you had for the other corners (20 pixels) and click OK. Instant rounded corner!

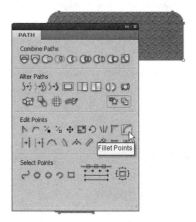

Figure 35b The Path panel offers many features not available before in Fireworks, including the Fillet Points command, to easily curve a hard-corner point.

9. Repeat the process for the other corner.

The Path panel opens up many possibilities for creative design, even if you are not a whiz with the Pen tool. You can punch out corners, punch out holes in a shape, and apply a combination of patterns, textures, or Live Filters for a realistic look, and suddenly you aren't just dealing with a plain old vector any more (**Figure 35c**).

Enter Name

Figure 35c Punching out shapes and applying patterns and Live Filters can totally transform a plain vector.

#36 Understanding the Pen Tool

The most commonly used vector tools are the Text, Shape, and Pen tools. Designers are always adding text to designs, be it just for mock-ups or for actual headings. Most designs contain elements to hold other objects like text and graphics, and when these standard shapes aren't enough, you can turn to the Pen tool to create your own custom vector shapes or paths.

Of the three tools mentioned, the least understood tool is probably the Pen tool.

The Pen tool let's you create custom shapes and paths by drawing with the mouse. It also allows you to edit existing shapes by adding anchor points. Unlike the Pencil bitmap tool, where you basically just click and drag to draw a bitmap line, using the Pen tool involves clicking the mouse to set a straight line between two anchor points (a place where the path can change direction) or clicking and dragging to create a curved section of a path (**Figure 36a**). Basically, every time you want to change the direction of a path, you move the mouse to the desired position and then click the left mouse button to set an anchor point.

Figure 36a Click to set a straight path or click and drag to turn the path into a curve.

As you add more anchor points, Fireworks displays the path outline in blue. To stop using the Pen tool, do one of the following:

- Close the path (create a shape) by clicking on the original starting anchor point (**Figure 36b**).

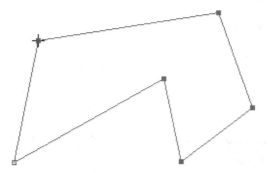

Figure 36b Closing a path to create a shape.

- Double-click on the last anchor point to create an open path (**Figure 36c**).

Figure 36c Double-clicking on the last created anchor point will disengage the Pen tool.

After a path is created, you can use the Subselection tool to select and alter the location of individual anchors, thus changing the shape of the path.

To further alter the path, you can add more anchor points after the fact. Just select the Pen tool and click on the path where you want the new anchor point to appear.

Anchor points have two states: straight and curved. You can convert a straight point to a curved point by using the Pen tool to click and drag out the curve control arms, also known as Bezier control arms.

To convert a curved anchor to a straight point, just click on it once with the Pen tool. Click a second time to delete the anchor point entirely.

If you want to delete a straight anchor point, select it with the Subselection tool and press the Delete key.

Note
Many of these operations—adding anchors, deleting anchors, and so on—are also available in the new Path panel.

#37 Masking an Image with a Vector Shape

Controlling Object Transparency with a Mask

Mask transparency is controlled by the color of the fill. White fill produces a completely transparent mask. A black fill gives you a fill that is opaque. Grayscale allows you to control the opacity of the mask by moving in increments between white and black. Any shade of gray in between black and white will create a semitransparent effect. Light gray means the masked object will be slightly see-through. Dark gray means the object will be almost completely invisible inside the mask.

Vector masking is one of Fireworks most powerful features. It is a nondestructive way of cropping a bitmap image, where both the bitmap and vector remain editable after the mask has been applied. Compared to bitmap masks, vector masks tend to have a higher degree of control and accuracy because you use a path, not a brush, to create them. It's easy to change the fill or stroke of a vector mask. Generating the same type of effect with a bitmap mask can be more time consuming.

Vector masks use one of two modes: Path Outline or Grayscale Appearance. In Path Outline mode, the vector mask acts like a cookie cutter, using the shape of the path to act as the mask.

In Grayscale Appearance, any bitmap information in the vector's fill gets converted to an alpha channel and fades the image accordingly. The Creative command Auto Vector Mask works in this way.

You will find both modes in the Property Inspector.

Whether you have drawn a vector shape using a tool from the Tools panel or have used the Pen tool to create your own custom shape, you can easily apply it as a mask to an existing bitmap or even another vector.

To mask a bitmap with a vector, draw the vector shape and position it over the top of the image. The image information outside the shape will be hidden when the mask is applied. You can apply the mask in a few ways.

Method 1 :

1. Select both objects.

2. Select Modify > Mask > Group as Mask.

This method automatically sets the mask to Grayscale Appearance mode, so if your vector was set to any color but white, you'll notice that the image is semitransparent. To get a solid appearance, switch to Path Outline or select the mask in the Layers panel and change the Fill color to white.

Method 2:

1. Select the vector only.

2. Cut the vector shape (Ctrl/Command+X).

3. Select the image.

4. Select Edit > Paste as Mask.

This method automatically sets the mask to Path Outline regardless of the Fill color or style.

Method 3:

1. Select the image.

2. Cut the image from the canvas.

3. Select the vector.

4. Select Edit > Paste Inside.

The end result is identical to Method 2.

Once the image is masked you will see an image and a mask thumbnail in the Layers panel (**Figure 37a**).

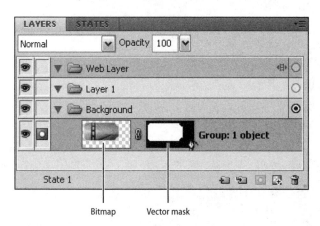

Bitmap   Vector mask

Figure 37a A bitmap image masked by a vector shape.

On the canvas you can reposition the image within the mask by using the Pointer tool and dragging the small blue *fleur* in the center of the image. You can also break the link between the image and the mask by clicking the chain link icon in the Layers panel.

Adding to a Vector Mask

You're not stuck with just one vector shape when you apply a mask. You can draw other shapes and add them to the original mask. Draw the new shape. Cut it from the canvas. Select the bitmap thumbnail (not the vector mask thumbnail) in the Layers panel. Select Edit > Paste as Mask and choose to either add the new shape to the mask or replace the original mask with the new shape.

Warning: My experience with this process is that you lose the ability to edit the vector anchor points after the mask has been deselected. The only way to edit the points is to ungroup the mask from the bitmap.

By selecting Show Fill and Stroke, you can experiment with a variety of custom edges with the Stroke options, even by just choosing some of the more abstract Stroke categories such as Oil, Random, or (my personal favorite) Unnatural. The possibilities are endless, so give some of the options a try. **Figures 37b, 37c, 37d**, and **37e** show a few creative examples.

Figure 37b Soft stroke creates a border around the masked image.

Figure 37c Changing the Stroke type (Stroke > Unnatural > Viscous Alien Paint) results in a completely different look.

Figure 37d The Outline Stroke type creates an interesting framing effect.

Figure 37e The anchor points of the vector mask can still be edited using the Subselection or Pen tool, giving you many creative options.

Tip
Tired of the mask entirely? No problem. Press Ctrl/Command+Shift+G or select Modify > Ungroup to separate the two objects.

Move the Image or Mask by Switching Tools
With the Pointer tool selected, dragging the little blue fleur will move the image around within the mask. If you switch to the Subselection tool, moving the fleur will drag the *mask* around.

Editing a Vector Mask
After a vector mask has been applied, you can use the Subselection tool to edit the anchor points of the mask. Make sure the vector mask thumbnail is selected in the Layers panel, and then use the Subselection tool to change the location of individual anchor points.

If you used an Auto Shape for the mask, you can either use the Pointer tool on the yellow control diamonds or convert the Auto Shape to a standard vector. To do this, however, you first must ungroup the image and the mask.

#38 Using the Auto Vector Mask for Quick Fades

You learned how to create a mask using a mask shape or a custom shape, but what if you just need to fade an image quickly? For example, you might need to fade a banner image at the top of a Web page to the background color of the Web site. The answer is to select Commands > Creative > Auto Vector Mask (**Figure 38a**). You can select a bitmap image or even another vector shape and quickly apply this command.

You can choose from eight preset gradient fade options, all of which are completely customizable after they have been applied.

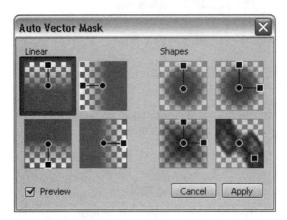

Figure 38a In previous versions of Fireworks, the Auto Vector Mask command was known as the Fade Image command. This updated version now allows for instant preview of the effect on the canvas.

After Auto Vector Mask has been applied, a vector shape completely covers the dimensions of the masked object. The vector mask is filled with a grayscale gradient (white is opaque, gray is semitransparent, and black is invisible). You can select the vector mask thumbnail in the Layers panel to activate the gradient control arms. By moving the control arms, you change the angle and transition of the fade. For a greater degree of control over the control arms, position the cursor over the arm rather than the start or end control anchors. When the cursor is in position, it will change to a rotate icon, as shown in **Figure 38b**.

Figure 38b Using your mouse to drag the control arm gives you finer control over the angle of the gradient. You can shorten the gradient (so it fades quicker) by dragging the square control handle or reposition the gradient by dragging the round control handle.

CHAPTER FIVE

Working with Multiple Images

Sometimes all you need to do is tweak, correct, or optimize an image, but as Web designers, more often you will be designing a Web site mock-up or be combining images to create a brand-new illustration or visual concept. Fireworks helps you work with multiple images in many ways. In this chapter you'll learn a few methods for arranging and aligning images.

#39 Name Your Objects

As you start to work with more than a single image or object within a design, it's a good idea to name your objects so they are easy to locate and organize within the Fireworks document.

Fireworks has several levels of organization available: pages, Web layers, Web sublayers, hotspots, slices, layers, sublayers, states, and image objects and groups. With the exception of the main Web layer, all these elements can be renamed by the user.

You can use pages to create unique designs or layouts independent of other pages. This is great for creating concepts and design variations, and for generating an interactive click-through.

Hotspots and slices are used for creating interactive features such as hyperlinks or rollovers.

Layers, sublayers, and groups can be used to organize design content based on function, similarity, object type, or any other way you feel makes sense to you.

States can be used for representing different visual states of an inter-face design or for rollover effects.

To rename any of the aforementioned elements, just locate the default name in the appropriate panel (Web layers, standard layers, and image objects are found in the Layers panel, states in the States panel, etc.), double-click on the name and then type in a new name (**Figure 39**).

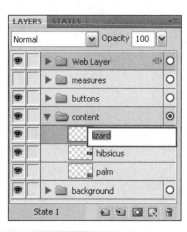

Figure 39 Get into the habit of naming your elements. The names will be very handy when you revisit a design down the road and when exporting files.

Page, hotspot, and slice names need to be treated with some care, because these names will be used in any resulting HTML and images export. So avoid spaces or special characters in their names. It's best to keep the names simple and perhaps use all lowercase letters for these names.

#**40** Using Guides for Alignment

As mentioned in Chapter 1, "Getting Started," you can use several methods to help you lay out a design. Guides have been available in many previous versions of Fireworks. They are especially useful for creating a wire frame for a design. You can drag vertical guides in to a blank canvas to set column widths and drag horizontal guides to set the heights for specific areas, such as a header, content divs, and footers.

Note

To use guides, you must first make the rulers visible (View > Rulers)

Figure 40a shows a blank canvas and dragged on guides to help "block out" a design. With Tooltips active, you will see exact pixel dimensions as you drag guides into place.

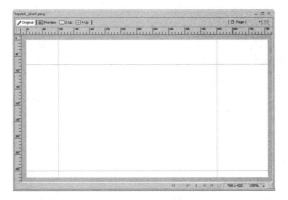

Figure 40a You can use guides to "wire frame" your design at the start.

To help you draw vectors, add guides around the perimeter of the design (**Figure 40b**). They will help the shape "snap" to your starting corner, even if you're not exactly at the 0,0 position.

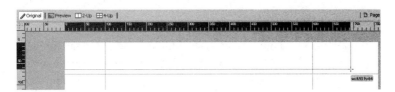

Figure 40b Setting up guides around the perimeter of your design can help when drawing full-width vector shapes. This figure also shows how Tooltips provide a live update of the dimensions of the vector shape.

Cropping a Single Bitmap Image in a Design

One neat Fireworks' feature is the ability to crop a specific bitmap image easily. Select the image and choose Edit > Crop Selected Bitmap. A crop marquee appears around the image, and you can drag the control handles to create a new rectangular crop of the image. But keep in mind this is a permanent change to the image in your design (but not the original file). After you close the file, there will be no way to undo the crop.

Note

If you let go of a guide and it's not exactly in the right place, don't fiddle with the cursor to change the position. Just double-click on the guide and a dialog opens that allows you to set the pixel distance exactly.

With the rough layout set up using guides, you can start bringing images and other objects into the design.

To start, use a rectangle for the header. With Guides and Guide Snapping active, it's easy to draw a rectangle that is the correct size. Select the Rectangle tool. Start in the upper-left corner and drag to the right side. As you near the bottom corner of the Banner Guide, the shape will snap into place.

You can fill the rectangle with a basic Linear Gradient (select Fill Category > Gradient > Linear in the Property Inspector), or you can use any gradient, pattern, or solid color you like. You might even want to use an image for the header. This is a great opportunity to use the Import feature (File > Import), which was discussed briefly in Chapter 2, "Graphics Boot Camp." Let's put it into action!

If you have an image that is the correct width or larger, you can import the image into the current document. Choose File > Import and browse for your image.

When you select the image, you'll be brought back to Fireworks and the Import icon will appear (see Technique #15 in Chapter 2).

With guides visible and Snap to Guides active, the import cursor will snap to the guides as you click and drag. However, Smart Guides and Tooltips are not available when using the import cursor.

Note

When importing images, ensure that the image you are importing is large enough to meet your minimum height or width requirement. If you import an image that is smaller in pixel dimensions than your target area, sizing the image using the import cursor will most likely have a negative impact on the quality of the image.

If your image is imported at the right width but is too tall for your requirements, you can either crop the bitmap or use a vector shape to mask the bitmap. Cropping is permanent, so if you're not sure about the final design, masking may be a better choice. For more on vector masking, see Technique #37. To crop one image in an existing design, see the sidebar "Cropping a Single Bitmap Image in a Design."

Note

If you copy and paste an image with a print resolution that is different than your target document, Fireworks will ask you if you want to resample the image. However, when you import an image, Fireworks assumes you want to use the target document's resolution and just places the image where you click.

If the image you chose for the banner relates to the design, you can make some of or all of your primary design color choices by sampling the image.

If you are following along, you can use the same import process to bring in three small images on the right side. After you import the first one at the size you want, drag in vertical guides on either side of the photo. In this example, the width of the images is important to the design (**Figure 40c**). Select File > Import and browse for your additional files. The standard guides help you keep objects in line and at the right dimension.

Figure 40c The Import icon is "guide aware" and snaps your imported image to the nearest guides as you drag the mouse.

Adobe Kuler for Color Selection

Make your design color selection easy by using Adobe Kuler. You can use the kuler panel in Fireworks (see Technique #77). Just go to http://kuler.adobe.com and sign in. You can choose from hundreds (if not thousands) of color themes. You can also create your own. A favorite method of mine is to upload a photo to kuler or link to my flickr site (www.flickr.com/ jim_babbage) via kuler. You can also check out a couple of my online tutorials at Community MX for details on using the Web version of kuler (http://tinyurl.com/ 55kavl). Kuler is also available as a desktop AIR application. You can find out more at http://kuler. adobe.com.

#**41** Using the Align Panel

Guides can help you with dimensions and location of objects, but unless you drag in several guides, they won't be much help when you are trying to evenly space a series of objects vertically or horizontally.

Enter the Align panel.

By default, the Align panel assumes you want to align objects relative to each other. If you want to align objects in relation to the canvas, select the Position icon in the upper-right corner of the panel.

Select all the objects you want to space evenly. Open the Align panel (**Figure 41a**), which by default is grouped with the Optimize panel. If your top and bottom (or left and right) objects are in the correct locations, you can use either the appropriate Distribute command in the Align panel or the Space command. If you are just dragging objects around the canvas and they haven't been lined up horizontally or vertically, you can use the Top, Right, Bottom, or Left alignment buttons.

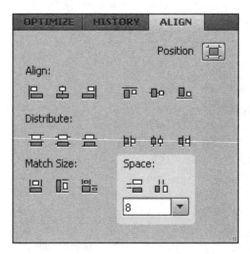

Figure 41a Like all panels, the Align panel has been updated visually, but it also includes new functionality in how you control the horizontal or vertical space between selected objects.

A new feature in the Align panel allows you to set a *pixel value* for the space between the selected objects. The standard space evenly setting calculates the space between objects based on the *y* axis locations of the objects farthest apart (*x* axis for horizontally spaced images). But this functionality may not give you the spacing you want. Setting a pixel value will force a specific gap between each selected object, even if it means the objects are spread farther apart on the canvas.

Aligning vector control handles (anchors) is now more intuitive, too. If you use the Subselection tool to select a specific anchor, the Align panel automatically changes to show you align options for the anchors (**Figure 41b**). In previous versions of Fireworks, you had to manually select this option.

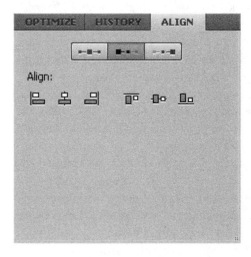

Figure 41b Access to aligning individual vector anchors is now automatic as soon as you use the Subselection tool to select one or more anchors.

#42 Grouping Images

Once you have your elements in position, grouping them together can make it easy to reposition multiple objects or just show and hide them at will. This feature is helpful for organizing related objects. For example, you might have several elements that make up a header or a series of images (photos or buttons) that need to maintain their physical position in relation to each other but may still need to be moved around the canvas to a new location.

Select the objects you want to keep as a group, either by Shift-clicking the objects directly on the canvas or Shift-clicking in the Layers panel (Control-click if the objects in the Layers panel are not already directly above or below each other). Select Modify > Group or press Ctrl/Command+G. When you create a group, it is assigned a new, generic name by Fireworks, but you can double-click on this name in the Layers panel to change it, just as you would for individual objects.

If you have applied Live Filters to the different objects within a group, those effects are maintained, but you won't see the Live Filters within the Property Inspector. To edit them, you will need to use the Subselection tool to activate an object within the group.

If you apply Live Filters to the group, those effects will be lost if you ungroup the objects.

To ungroup objects, select Modify > Ungroup or press Ctrl/Command+Shift+G. The objects will break apart in the Layers panel, and the original object names will display next to the thumbnails.

Figure 42 shows the final roughed out design, including bitmaps—some of which are masked—as well as pattern-filled vector shapes.

Figure 42 Guides, groups, and the Align panel help make quick work of an initial mock-up.

CHAPTER SIX

The Big Picture on Web Graphics

First and foremost, Fireworks is a graphics application for creating and editing Web graphics. It performs many other tasks as well, especially in CS4, but the Web is still its primary focus—be it for creating mock-ups, editing screen resolution images, exporting graphics to Flash, or optimizing and exporting to CSS and HTML.

In Chapter Two, "Graphics Boot Camp," you learned some of the basics for working with graphics in Fireworks. The techniques in this chapter focus on the Web.

When it comes to Web workflow, Fireworks designers are split into two camps: those who use it to create stunning designs or edit graphics, and then use other applications such as Dreamweaver or a text editor to code their HTML, and those who want the same creativity and ease of use, but also want Fireworks to generate their HTML.

For quite some time, the latter group was not fulfilled because Fireworks seemed trapped in the world of table-based layouts. While this style of design can be handy for quickly generating a click-through HTML prototype, Fireworks' table-based layouts were very rigid and did not allow for any deviation or future editing in the HTML without causing a lot of damage to the design. Also, Fireworks' table-based designs tended to be fairly inaccessible (all graphics, all the time). The tables and the spacer GIFs could be a nightmare to deal with when maintaining the site, too.

But Fireworks has taken another step forward in CS4 with the inclusion of a new export option called CSS and Images. This new export script exports standards-based CSS and HTML. So in theory you can now generate a proper Web page from within Fireworks. Technique #46 covers this in more detail.

If you want to produce compositions that will make their way into a Web page, you'll need to be familiar with Fireworks' Web tools. The Web tools included in the Tools panel consist of four main icons:

- Hotspot tool
- Slice tool
- Show Hotspots and Slices
- Hide Hotspots and Slices

#**43** Interactivity Using the Hotspot Tool

The Hotspot tool is one of two Web-centric tools in the Tools panel (**Figure 43a**). It's used to create one or several hyperlinks within a single, unsliced graphic. It is most commonly used for image maps for Web site navigation.

Figure 43a The Web tools have their own section in the Tools panel.

Hotspots have other uses as well. From an HTML perspective, you can use them to trigger a disjointed (or remote) rollover. This is a situation where the user clicks or mouses over one area and another area on the page changes. This interactivity is typically done with JavaScript (and at the time of this writing still is done this way), but there are CSS methods for doing this also. However, because they don't involve Fireworks, they will not be covered here.

You can use the Rectangle Hotspot tool when creating an interactive PDF (see the sidebar "Making Interactive PDFs" in Chapter Two.)

The Hotspot tool consists of three tools: Rectangle, Circle, and Polygon (**Figure 43b**). You can quickly access the tool by pressing the J key. Like all multiple tool icons in the Tools panel, if you keep pressing the shortcut key (or hold down the left mouse button on the tool), you will toggle through all the available tools.

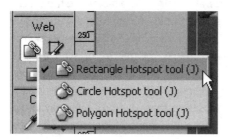

Figure 43b You can also click and hold on the current tool icon to trigger a pop-up menu.

The Rectangle and Circle Hotspots tools are pretty self-explanatory and produce fairly simple HTML code. With the Polygon Hotspot tool you can create precise hotspot shapes around irregularly shaped objects. But the amount of HTML markup this type of hotspot produces is significant, so it's best to use the Polygon Hotspot tool sparingly.

Tip

Dreamweaver's Property Inspector can also create image maps in a similar fashion. Just select the image, and the image map tools become available at the lower left of the Property Inspector.

To create a hotspot, select the Hotspot tool icon or press J to jump to that tool set. The Rectangle Hotspot tool is the default. Move your cursor into your design and draw a box that encompasses the clickable area for your hotspot. When you release the mouse button, the Property Inspector (**Figure 43c**) changes to reflect attributes for the hotspot. You can add a URL (absolute or relative), Alt text, and a hotspot title, and even change the shape of the hotspot. Hotspots can't change the state of the image applied to them as in a standard rollover image, however.

Figure 43c You can name a hotspot and set interactivity in the Property Inspector.

Tip

If you are adding a link to an external Web site, you must include the full URL, for example, http://www.peachpit.com. Links to pages or images within the same local folder can be set as relative links (e.g., contact.html or bigPicture.jpg).

If the size of the hotspot is incorrect, you can use the Pointer tool to first select the hotspot, and then drag one of the anchor points to increase or reduce the size of the hotspot.

After a hotspot is created it will also display in the Layers panel in the Web layer. You can name each hotspot by double-clicking on the default name in the Layers panel. If your goal is to use the hotspots on a Web page, avoid names with spaces or special characters.

Note

Hotspots are used just for interactivity. Adding a hotspot will not cut up the image into smaller pieces on export or give you the ability to set custom file settings or turn the image underneath the hotspot into a rollover effect. Those features are handled by the Slice tool.

#44 Sliced Images for Custom Optimization

Slicing a design or image gives you the power to customize the file format and compression settings for each slice element. This is referred to as *optimizing* an image. Without slices your image or design can only have one optimization setting applied to it. As you'll see in Technique #45, like hotspots, slices can also have interactivity added to them, such as image rollovers, hyperlinks, and remote rollovers.

You can create a slice in a couple of ways: You can use the Slice or Polygon Slice tool found in the Web tools section of the Tools panel. Or, you can right-click/Control-click on the image (**Figure 44a**) you want to slice, and then choose the slice style you want from the context menu (hotspots can also be created in this manner).

Figure 44a Right-clicking on an object will launch a context menu.

After a slice is applied to an image, you can use the Optimize panel to set the file format and compression settings for the image area under the selected slice. (You can also view and set default optimizations using the drop-down menu in the Property Inspector.)

Note
With the exception of button symbols, a slice object is not attached to the image below it, so if you reposition the image, you also need to reposition the slice.

The Optimize panel is located by default in the topmost panel group in the panel dock. If you don't see it, select Window > Optimize to bring it to the forefront (**Figure 44b**). It let's you choose the graphic file format you would like to use when exporting a selected slice. Each slice in a design can have completely different optimization settings, which allow for a high level of control over a Web page's *page weight*. By following the guidelines in the sidebar "Web File Formats—Choosing JPEG, GIF, or PNG" and by making liberal use of the Preview, 2-Up, or 4-Up views, you can determine an appropriate file format and compression setting for each slice in the design.

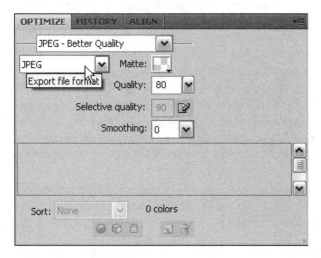

Figure 44b The Optimize panel gives you complete control over file settings for a sliced image.

You can set basic Web optimization settings for a slice using the Property Inspector, but you will get much more control in the Optimize panel. It's also worth noting that the Optimize panel gives you the ability to choose non-Web formats such as TIFF and BMP, in case your designs—or elements of it—are destined for other uses.

Any changes you make to the optimization settings in either the Property Inspector or the Optimize panel will *only* apply to the selected slice (or slices). If no slices are selected, the settings will apply to all unsliced areas of the design.

If you've created a slice over a photo, choose JPEG from the Export File Format menu. Then switch to the Preview view and try out different quality settings until you find that balance between small file size and acceptable quality.

For more on the Web optimization process, see Techniques #47 and #48.

Showing and Hiding Web Elements

The two other tools in the Web tool set are for showing or hiding hotspots and slices. As you start adding Web features to your design, it can be difficult to select the images beneath for additional editing. You can use the Select Behind tool (grouped with the Pointer tool), but hiding the slices and hotspots makes it much easier to see your design and alter the image objects, be they text, bitmaps, or vectors. (You can also reveal and hide Web elements in the Web Layer of the Layers panel.)

Web File Formats—Choosing JPEG, GIF, or PNG

To a degree, the file format you choose is a subjective choice, but here are some general guidelines:

JPEG. For photographic images, JPEG format gives you photorealistic (32-bit) color, and you can control the quality and compression of the file. Higher quality means less compression, which in turn means a larger file size. JPEG is also a *lossy* format, meaning that each time a JPEG file is saved, more of the original image data is discarded. Try to edit files in a nonlossy format such as PNG, TIFF, or PSD, and then save/export the final file as a JPEG if a JPEG is required. (JPEG is also used when a composition includes gradients or shadows.)

GIF. The GIF format is limited to 256 colors (8-bit), but these colors are customizable. That said, GIF tends to be best for images with solid color, such as logos, line art, or text-based graphics. The GIF format supports transparency settings (indexed transparency) that can give your image the impression of floating over the top of another image or colored background. GIF supports frame-based animation so you can create simple Web graphic animations. For complex or large animations, consider using Flash.

PNG. The PNG format tries to give you the best of both worlds: You can choose among 32-bit, 24-bit, and 8-bit PNG. A 32-bit PNG allows for 24-bit photorealistic color with 8-bit *alpha transparency* so you can get more realistic drop shadows or glows around an image, or even make the image appear semitransparent on the Web page. The image will blend seamlessly with the background color of the Web page. Internet Explorer 6 and earlier require special JavaScript to render alpha transparency. A 24-bit PNG is mildly compressed and lossless, meaning that no image data is discarded when the file is saved. However, unlike JPEG files, you cannot control the compression or quality. The file size is what it is. An 8-bit PNG is much like a GIF but does not support frame-based animation. Often, you will get smaller file sizes by exporting as PNG-8 rather than GIF. It's definitely worth testing.

Fireworks uses a modified version of the PNG format as its native file format, giving you a great deal of flexibility for editing files. This modified format contains information about layers, frames, and effects, and as a result, is a much larger file size than a standard flattened PNG file. Avoid using the Fireworks PNG as part of the real Web page for this reason. If you want to use the PNG format, the three settings listed above will export like other image formats.

#45 Slice Images for Interactivity

Much like hotspots, you can add hyperlinks to slices. If you export Fireworks HTML, those URLs remain with the images. If you export an interactive PDF, again, those links will remain with the slices.

Slices can become *rollover images* but hotspots cannot. Because a slice is basically a chopped up part of a large image, you can use built-in JavaScript behaviors within Fireworks to set up a *swap image behavior*. JavaScript rollovers are common in navigation bars. Although the use of CSS and background images is quickly becoming more popular, JavaScript rollovers are quick and easy to do when creating a graphical Web site click through. In this manner, you can easily show a client all the visual interactivity using JavaScript for the mock up, and then deal with coding the CSS rollovers later for the production site.

Here's how to create a simple rollover effect:

1. Create a new document.

2. Draw a rectangle shape on the canvas and fill it with a color.

3. Open the States panel (formerly the Frames panel). Right-click on State 1 and choose Duplicate State (**Figure 45a**). When the Duplicate State dialog appears, click OK to accept the defaults.

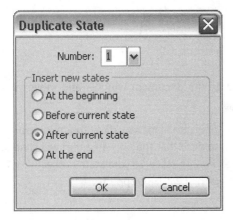

Figure 45a Duplicate State panel.

You now have two identical graphics in two separate states.

(continued on next page)

Fireworks as a Web Page Creation Tool

There is a vocal camp that consists of users who scoff at graphics editors that try to be HTML page creators. But there is a place for this feature. I use Fireworks' standard HTML capabilities for creating graphical HTML click throughs for client feedback. After prototype approval, I then code the pages using Dreamweaver. Fireworks is incredibly fast and easy to use from a creation and editing standpoint. It's a great way to test ideas without having to code right away. The client can request changes on the visual aspects of the site, and you don't have to write a single line of HTML code. Just update the design in Fireworks and export again.

If it's so great, why not use it for the final site? Herein lies the issue. Fireworks' rollovers (simple, complex, or remote) are created using both a table-based layout and JavaScript. You should try to use more modern techniques that employ CSS whenever possible because you will have a much easier time maintaining your site and editing it in the future. From a best practices perspective, try to avoid table-based layouts.

4. Select the rectangle in State 2 and change the color.

5. Go to State 1. On the canvas, right-click on the rectangle and choose Insert Rectangular Slice. A slice will be created, matching the dimensions of the rectangle.

6. Click on the behavior handle (small circle in the middle of the slice) and select Add Simple Rollover Behavior (**Figure 45b**).

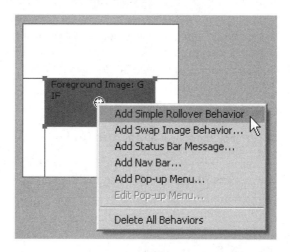

Figure 45b Behaviors can be applied to slices or hotspots and use JavaScript to run within a Web page.

7. Select the Preview view in the document window and move your mouse over the rectangle.

Presto-chango! You can apply this same workflow to any object on the canvas. It's important to note that the only area that will change on the rollover is the area under the slice. So your State 2 object should be the same size as the slice, or it will be cropped.

#46 Creating a Remote Rollover

Now you can take what you've learned about hotspots and slices and put it into practice. For reference, the technique numbers are provided for everything you do in this exercise.

1. If you've been building a sample design as you go through this chapter, you can work with that file or create a new empty document. If you're starting fresh, create a document (#1) that is at least 600 pixels wide by 400 pixels high.

2. Import (#15) a couple of images (if you haven't done so already) or draw a couple of rectangle shapes (#31). Move them off to the right side of your canvas and make sure they are not too large (no more than 150 pixels wide—#40). One image should be above the other on the canvas.

3. Align the images vertically using Smart Guides or Guides (#7, #40), or the Align panel (#41). Name each object based on its subject matter (#39).

4. Right-click on each image and choose Insert Rectangular Hotspot (#43). Name the hotspots **thumb1** and **thumb2** respectively (#39). As soon as you add a hotspot, the Web features should become visible on the canvas. If they don't, click the Show Hotspots and Slices icon in the Tools panel.

5. Create two duplicate states of the layer in which your objects are contained (#45). Name these new States **zoom1** and **zoom2** (#39).

6. Select the States panel and make zoom1 the active state. Import the same image as the one under the thumb1 hotspot but at a larger dimension. Position it somewhere near the middle of the canvas without overlapping the thumbnails. Name the newly imported image **Large** (*subject matter*).

7. Right-click on the image and choose Insert Rectangular Slice. Use the Optimize panel to set the slice to JPEG – Better Quality and name the slice **zoom_image** (#44 and #39). Make a note of the slice's dimensions by checking the Property Inspector.

8. Go to the zoom2 state and import the image matching the thumb2 hotspot. Size it so the image is no larger than the slice created for the prior image. Do not add a slice to this image.

(continued on next page)

9. You should now have three states; the original state plus the two new states. You can toggle through them by clicking on each state in the States panel or by choosing the state from the States menu at the bottom left of the Layers panel (**Figure 46a**).

Figure 46a After states are created, you can select them from the Layers panel.

10. Here's the fun part! Go to the first state, click on the behaviors handle, and choose Add Swap Image Behavior (#45). The Swap Image dialog (**Figure 46b**) appears. Select the zoom slice from the left column. In the State no. drop-down list choose zoom1 (2). Click OK.

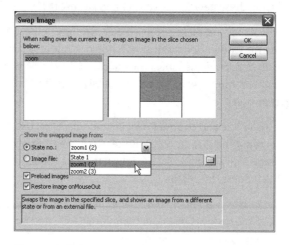

Figure 46b The Swap Image dialog is your control center for creating remote rollover effects.

11. Select the second hotspot and repeat the process, choosing zoom2 (3) this time.

12. Save the file. You can now test the rollover in a couple of different ways:

- Click the Preview view. You should see a different zoomed image appear as you mouse over each of the two thumbnails.

- Select File > Preview in Browser > Preview in *default browser* or press F12 when mocking up an AIR application prototype.

The total number of different essential techniques used for this exercise is nine, and several of these were used multiple times.

Exporting Images—Quality vs. File Size

A primary goal for Web images is to keep the file sizes small yet maintain quality. High-speed Internet connections are more common, but there are still many users on dial-up or shared connections. For truly global Web sites, page weight should still be a concern.

Images are normally viewed on the Web at 100% magnification, which means:

- Export Web images at the desired pixel dimensions for the Web page. (Don't export large files and scale them down in your Web editor. The large file is still downloaded to the viewer's computer. The browser then rescales the image to a smaller size.)

- Optimize images to look acceptable at 100% magnification.

Test the files using one of the Preview options. The Preview views in the main document window are indispensable and are there to let you test different formats or compression/quality settings.

All metadata is discarded when you *export* files because you usually export files for use on the Web. Metadata adds to the file size, so it is excluded. To maintain metadata, choose File > Save As and choose a suitable format.

#47 Optimize Panel and Preview Views

What the Heck is Matte Color?

Matte color is available in all the export formats and is the color Fireworks uses on all areas of the canvas not covered by an object. Typically, changing the canvas color of the document will update the matte color to match, but you can also change the matte color independently in the Matte color box without affecting the original canvas color. This can be very handy if you need to export the same graphic for use on a variety of Web page background colors. Matte color also comes into play when you are exporting a GIF or PNG with a transparent background for overlay onto a colored background.

As a Web designer, the Optimize panel is one of your main production tools. Whether you are exporting a single image or multiple slices from a fully rendered page design, you'll turn to the Optimize panel to tweak those graphics. Interestingly enough, this panel is only one of several optimization workflows you can utilize.

The sidebar "Web File Formats—Choosing JPEG, GIF, or PNG," discussed the main file formats used by Web browsers and how to decide which format to use for specific types of images or goals. In Technique #44, you looked at slicing and its relationship to optimization. Now you'll learn how the Optimize panel and the various Preview modes work together.

Open a file and try each of the previews. By default, Fireworks starts in *Original* view, a single document window for a single image file. In this view you can edit the image, add hotspots, add slices, and so on. When you choose Preview, 2-Up, or 4-Up views, you'll see how your optimization settings affect the exported file or slice.

Which view you choose depends on your preferred workflow. If you want a quick, full-window view of your optimization settings, use the Preview mode. If you want to do some comparative testing, choose 2-Up or ideally 4-Up because the document window is split into smaller windows. Each window shows its own optimization settings. The 2-Up view shows you by default the Original view and one export view. The 4-Up view (**Figure 47a**) quarters the document window and displays the Original view plus three export views. You can customize the optimization settings of each window by selecting it and changing properties in the Optimize panel. You can compare how the same image would look as a JPEG or GIF file, or how JPEG 80 quality, JPEG 45 quality, and JPEG 60 quality would affect the file size and detail of the same image.

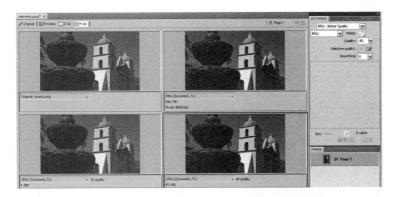

Figure 47a Use the 4-Up view to compare different optimization settings.

The Optimize panel is context sensitive. As you change export formats, the panel updates for that specific format. JPEG (**Figure 47b**) only has options for Matte color, Quality, Selective Quality, and Smoothing.

Figure 47b The Optimize panel displaying the JPEG attributes.

GIF, Animated GIF, and PNG 8 (**Figure 47c**) have options for Matte color, Indexed Palette type, number of colors, Loss, Dither, and Transparency.

N-Up

If you use the N-Up feature (multiple document windows that are docked to the application frame), each document window will sport its own Original, Preview, 2-Up, and 4-Up views.

Save Optimization Settings

If you create a custom optimization setting, you can save it for use at a later time. Click the Options button and choose Save Settings.

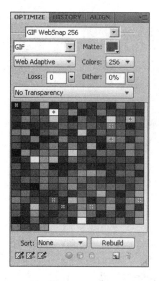

Figure 47c The Optimize panel displaying GIF attributes.

PNG 24 and 32 have no user controls other than Matte color.

The Optimize panel options (**Figure 47d**) contain several features and actions not available in the panel, such as the ability to choose interlacing for GIF files, or Progressive JPEG. You also have quick access to the Export Wizard and the Optimize to Size command.

Figure 47d Most panels have additional options that you can access from the Options button at the right side of the gray tab bar of the panel. The options will differ depending on which panel is currently active.

The Big Picture on Web Graphics

#**48** Creating Slices Manually with the Slice Tool

To slice an *entire* object, you can use the right-click option to create slices quickly and easily. But there will be many times when you only want or need to slice segments of an object.

You can choose from two slice tools: Rectangle and Polygon. Because Web pages are essentially laid out in a grid format, you will most often use the Rectangle Slice tool. The Polygon Slice tool can be useful if you want a nonrectangular area to be interactive, but this tool uses HTML tables and hotspots as well as slices (the resulting exported file consists of rectangular slices in a table and a polygon hotspot). You can't have polygon-shaped images, just like you can't have elliptical-shaped images on a Web page. Like it or not, everything ends up as a rectangle (because HTML *only* records width and height for an object in a Web page). If you use a lot of polygon slices, your HTML code can become quite complex and require more browser processing time. I can honestly say I've never had a reason to use the Polygon Slice tool.

Figure 48a shows a rounded rectangle. By the time this rectangle becomes part of an HTML page, chances are you'll want the rectangle to be flexible enough to expand or contract depending on the content within it. Exporting the shape as a single slice won't give you that kind of flexibility. Instead, you need to slice it into three pieces: a top, middle, and bottom.

Figure 48a Rounded rectangle vector shape.

Accurate slicing is important, so follow these steps:

1. Zoom in to clearly see the edges of the rectangle (**Figure 48b**).

2. Set up Guides along each side of the object. This can be helpful because the Slice tool will snap to Guides.

3. Select the Slice tool.

4. Draw a rectangular slice over the top portion of the rounded rectangle. This slice should include the full radius of the corner and a couple of pixels worth of the straight vertical sides.

5. Release the mouse. The slice will display a basic name in the upper-left corner and the default export format. The slice will also appear in the Web layer of the Layers panel.

Figure 48b Zooming into the object can improve your accuracy when slicing an image.

If this is your first time creating a slice by hand, don't be surprised if you need to tweak the dimensions of the slice. You can double-check your slice width by selecting the rounded rectangle and seeing if the width in the Property Inspector matches the width of the slice. If you need to make adjustments, you can either use the Pointer tool to resize the slice or change the dimensions numerically in the Property Inspector.

As mentioned in #46, name your slice in either the Property Inspector or the Web layer. Its name becomes the final filename for the sliced graphic when you export the slice. If you don't name your slice, Fireworks uses an *auto naming* function, which generally creates a name that will not make sense to you a few days later. Avoid spaces and special characters in slice names. This is considered best practice for Web files and can eliminate some potential problems when the page is uploaded to a server.

If needed, change the optimization settings for your slice as well. You can make basic changes in the Property Inspector, or you can use the

Optimize panel for more control over format, compression, and even transparency (for GIFs and PNGs).

If necessary, select the Slice tool again. This time draw a very short slice to act as the middle segment of the rectangle. This particular image slice would become a repeating background image for the div or table cell representing your container. This slice only needs to be a few pixels high and as wide as the rectangle. Don't forget to name the slice.

The last slice will be for the bottom, but rather than slicing it manually, let's look at a couple of slice duplicating shortcuts!

Select the top slice again. Hold down the Alt/Option key and drag the slice. This creates a duplicate of the slice, just as Alt/Option would when used in conjunction with any other object. Drag the duplicate slice to the bottom of the rectangle and position it as desired. Smart Guides are helpful when positioning the new slice accurately.

You can also create a copy of the slice by pressing Control/Command+ Shift+D. Using either scenario, you will still need to name the slices you create, or Fireworks will generate a name automatically.

The three slices you made (**Figure 48c**) are the building blocks you need to create a visually expandable container for text or graphics on a Web page. You'll see slicing in action more in #85, "Exporting CSS and Images."

Figure 48c The rectangle with three slices completed.

#49 Working with Image Preview

You access Image Preview (**Figure 49**) by selecting File > Image Preview. It's essentially a smaller and separate all-in-one version of the Preview, 2-Up, and 4-Up views and is very handy for exporting your files in formats other than your main choice. For example, you might have sliced your entire design using multiple optimization settings for the various slices. But you also need to quickly export a flat JPEG or TIFF version of the entire design. Image Preview is at your service.

Figure 49 The Image Preview window is another way to optimize an image or part of an image.

You can use the preview tools to scroll around the design, zoom in or out, and even crop the image. The dialog is expandable as well; you can stretch it out to see your entire graphic.

The Options tab gives you control over file format and compression. The File tab shows you the scaling options for the full image and the export area controls based on the tool. The Animation tab will only be available if your export format is GIF animation.

After selecting the desired settings, click the Export button to pick a destination folder. When the Export dialog opens, you're given a final chance to change the export settings. This is the same dialog you would see if you selected File > Export.

Note
If you use Dreamweaver CS3 or CS4, you may have already met the Image Preview window. It appears when you try to insert a non-Web image format (PSD, TIFF, etc.) into a Web page.

#50 Using the Export Area Tool

As you've already learned, there are many ways to export images from Fireworks. Slices are handy if you have multiple image elements you need to export into a Web-ready format. But if you only need to grab a specific area of a design and don't want to bother with the whole slicing process, try using the Export Area tool. It behaves much like the Crop tool to begin with but doesn't change your original image in any way.

You can access the Export Area tool by pressing the C key or by clicking and holding on the Crop tool icon in the Tools panel. The Export Area cursor looks like an "L" shape with a tiny camera inside it (**Figure 50a**).

Figure 50a The Export Area cursor. The "L" shape is designed to help with accurate placement of the export area border.

Once selected, just click and drag over the area you want to export. You might use this tool to show a client a specific arrangement of images without having the entire page design in view. Or, you might just want to export the area as a different format such as TIFF. Just like the Crop tool, you can adjust the area by dragging the control handles (**Figure 50b**).

Figure 50b The Export Area tool behaves much like the Crop tool when selecting an area.

#50: Using the Export Area Tool

Need to Email a Sample Quickly?

The Send to Email feature is an often overlooked feature in Fireworks, yet it's been around since the first version. Selecting File > Send to Email gives you three ways to send your image: Fireworks PNG, JPEG Compressed, or Use Export Settings.

There is no intermediate dialog when you use this feature. Fireworks directly exports the file and attaches the image (or images) to a blank email ready to send.

Export Selected Slice(s) Using Context Menus

It happens: You've just exported your design and then realize that one sliced image needs some tweaking. You can easily export a single slice by right-clicking on the slice and choosing Export Selected Slice from the context menu. You can export multiple slices in the same manner by Shift-clicking the slices on the canvas. Release the Shift key and right-click just as before. Even though the menu still displays Slice, all the selected slices will be exported.

Exporting Multiple Pages

One power feature of Fireworks is the ability to create a multipage document. Each page can be distinct from the others, or they can share common elements via a Master Page or shared layer.

If you have a multipage document and want to export each page as a unique HTML page for a graphical click through or as a single interactive PDF, deselect the Current Page Only option in the Export dialog.

When you are satisfied, just double-click inside the area or press the Return/Enter key. This launches the Image Preview window, where you can set format and optimization settings just as you can in the Optimize panel.

Instead of just seeing the entire design as you would by choosing File > Image Preview, only the cropped area appears in the preview window (**Figure 50c**).

If you see an empty preview window, use the Hand tool to scroll around, or zoom out. Eventually, your export area will appear.

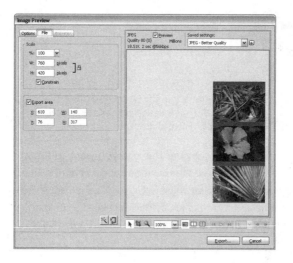

Figure 50c The Image Preview window with the selected area displayed.

Tip
To select an image area covered by a slice, you can either hide the slices using the Hide Slices and Hotspots icon in the Tools panel, or you can choose the Select Behind tool. It is located in the Pointer tool group and can also be accessed by pressing V or 0.

#51 Creating an Interactive Prototype

Export options have grown exponentially in Fireworks CS4. You looked at creating PDFs in Technique #22 and will be looking at exporting AIR prototypes in Technique #91 as well as exporting standards-compliant CSS and images in Technique #90. Here you'll explore an old standby option, export HTML and Images. This feature relies on using slices and/or hotspots, and will generate an image-based HTML table layout. While not particularly useful in terms of a final Web site (a lot of presentational markup is added to the HTML), it is a great way to elicit feedback and approvals from a client. The resulting Web page can have live links and rollover effects (standard and remote), and give the user a true sense of the functionality of a Web page design. Questions, comments, and changes can be addressed before time is spent coding the page in a Web editor such as Dreamweaver.

1. Click outside the canvas area to deselect any objects.

2. Set a default optimization of JPEG – Higher Quality in the Property Inspector. This setting will control how unsliced areas are exported.

3. Slice the objects you want to optimize. Remember to name your slices (even if this is not a final Web site, it can't hurt to get into the habit).

4. Add interactivity as needed, be it simple button rollovers or remote rollovers.

5. Select File > Export and choose HTML and Images as the Export type (**Figure 51a**). Make sure that Include Areas Without Slices is selected and that Selected Slices Only is deselected.

6. Because you're exporting a full-page mock-up, you'll need all the elements of the page regardless of whether you sliced them or not. So, also select the option Put images in subfolder.

Figure 51a The Export dialog offers many options including Adobe PDF, Images only, HTML and Images, and CSS and Images.

(continued on next page)

7. Before you click Save, click the Options button and select the Table tab (**Figure 51b**). Be sure that the "Space with" menu option chosen is either nested tables, no spacers, or 1 pixel transparent spacer.

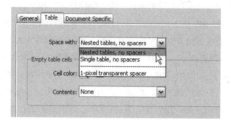

Figure 51b HTML options can be used to control aspects of the HTML export, such as how the HTML table should be constructed.

8. Set the Cell color to use canvas color and click OK.

9. Browse to the folder where you want the Web page and images saved. Click the Save button.

You can now launch a Web browser and open the HTML file. Mouse over your interactive areas to see how they respond based on your original Fireworks design. If you included any external hyperlinks as part of the design, they should also work.

In my project workflow, I'll complete an interactive prototype, which typically represents the top level navigation for the site. I upload that entire folder to my Web site, and then email the client with the URL to the index.htm page created by Fireworks and ask the client to test the design and comment on what the client sees.

CHAPTER SEVEN

Working with Type

Designers have had a love/hate relationship with type in Fireworks. Those who only used Fireworks tended to enjoy the simplicity of the Fireworks type engine, and in later versions, the ability to customize the anti-aliasing of text. Those who worked in other applications such as Photoshop and Illustrator were often frustrated with the incompatibility of type handling between Fireworks and other applications. Often, font attributes would be lost, and sometimes the entire font would be replaced when a user tried to edit the text. In addition, the font rendering produced by Fireworks was often not as crisp as you might get from a program like Photoshop, leaving text looking "muddy."

Many of these issues have been resolved in CS4 with the introduction of the Adobe Type Engine. The old Fireworks' type engines (and its modal text editor window) are gone now. As a result, you have much better consistency when bringing in PSD or AI files that contain text.

Text on a path created in Photoshop, for example, now remains editable *on* the path in Fireworks, and the type attributes are also maintained.

Aside from the improved text handling between applications, working with type can be a fun and creative part of your design, as you will see in the following techniques.

#52 Text Basics

Text appears inside a *text block* (a rectangle with handles). Text blocks are either *auto-sizing* or *fixed-width* blocks.

An auto-sizing text block expands horizontally as you type and shrinks when you remove text. Auto-sizing text blocks are created by default when you click on the canvas with the Text tool and start typing.

Fixed-width text blocks allow you to control the width of wrapped text. Fixed-width text blocks are created when you drag to draw a text block using the Text tool.

When the text pointer is active within a text block, a hollow square or hollow circle appears in the upper-right corner of the text block. The circle indicates an auto-sizing text block; the square indicates a fixed-width text block, as shown in **Figure 52a**. Double-click the corner to change from one text block to the other.

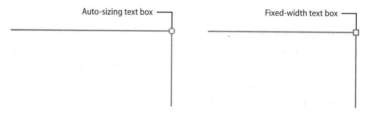

Figure 52a You can tell what type of text block you are working with by the shape of the handle in the upper-right corner of the text box.

When the Text tool is active, the Property Inspector displays attributes for formatting text, such as font family, font style, size (measured in points), color, alignment, tracking, leading, indent, horizontal scaling, text indent, and paragraph spacing (**Figure 52b**). You can also add a stroke color, stroke style, and Live Filters to text. You can change these settings before or after you have added text.

Figure 52b The Property Inspector is control central for changing the attributes of text.

To edit an existing text block, double-click in the text area with the Pointer tool or choose the Text tool and click once within the text area.

Typography Terms

Here are a few terms to know:

Kerning. Adjusts the space between letters based on character pairs. There is strong kerning (more space) between the letters V and A, and no kerning between letters S and T. Turn Auto kerning on or off in the Property Inspector.

Tracking. Unlike kerning, tracking adds equal amounts of space between all selected characters.

Leading. Also referred to as line spacing, leading is the amount of vertical spacing between lines of type.

Horizontal scaling. Adjusts the width of each selected character or characters within a selected text box.

Baseline shift. Controls how closely text sits above or below its natural baseline. For example, superscript text sits above the baseline. If there is no baseline shift, the text sits on the baseline. To adjust baseline shift, select the actual text (not the text box) and input a value into the Baseline Shift field in the Property Inspector.

Note

When you edit a text block, all changes during that edit session are considered to be a single undo.

Fireworks remembers the last font used by the Text tool, even after shut down and restart.

Tip

Holding down the Ctrl/Command key turns the Text tool into a Hand tool, allowing you to reposition the text block.

Tip

To insert special characters like a copyright or trademark symbol, set your cursor at the location in which you want to place the character, choose Window > Special Characters, and then select the character you want to use.

You can import text from a text file into Fireworks. To import text in RTF (rich text format) and ASCII (plain text) formats, copy it from the original text file and paste it into Fireworks. You can also select File > Open or File > Import and navigate to a file. (Imported ASCII text is set to the current fill color and default font of 12 pixels high; RTF text will retain its original formatting.)

For more information on the options for altering text, such as kerning, indenting, or leading, be sure to read the Fireworks Help files.

Live Font Preview

If you select a text box and go through the font family list, Fireworks shows you a preview (roughly, the first 15 characters) of how the selected text will appear when a particular font is chosen.

By default, Fireworks also shows the six most recently used fonts at the top of the list. You can change the number of recently used fonts in the list by going to the Preferences dialog. On Windows select Edit > Preferences > Type. On the Mac select Adobe Fireworks > Preferences > Type.

Controlling Text Orientation in a Text Box

Much like any word processor, you can control the alignment of text within a box by using the alignment buttons for left, right, centered, and justified text found in the Property Inspector. But you can also change the orientation of text from horizontal left to right to vertical right to left by clicking the Text Orientation button in the Property Inspector. You'll find this button just to the left of the alignment buttons.

#53 Using Type as a Mask

Many cool things can be done when you use text as a mask over a bitmap image or another vector. This technique works best with large type sizes and bold text like Arial Bold or Poster. Using text as a mask is easy!

1. Open an image file.

2. Type some text.

3. Make the font large—at least 40 pixels or more—and ideally bold.

4. Use the Pointer tool to select the text box and *cut* it from the canvas by pressing Ctrl/Command+X.

5. Select the bitmap image and choose Edit > Paste as Mask.

Instantly, only the area within the text will display the image. Like a standard mask, you can reposition the image by dragging the small blue *fleur,* or you can click the link between the image and the text mask to unlink them and move them around separately.

The greatest feature of this technique is that the text remains as text, so you can continue to edit it, change fonts, change the wording, and whatever else you like without having to ungroup the two objects (**Figure 53**).

Figure 53 You can still apply strokes to text when it is masked, and if you use a shade of gray for the stroke, you can add some interesting texture to the text.

Tip

When text is a mask, use the Text tool to make the text active and editable. To change the text size, style, or alignment, right-click/Control-click to access the text context menu. You can also access these options from the main Text menu.

Paste Inside

Another way to use text as a mask is to select Edit > Paste Inside. Type your text first (bold fonts tend to be best). Select the image you want the text to mask and cut the image from the canvas (Ctrl/Command+X). Select the text, and then choose Edit > Paste Inside.

Adding Depth to Text

Sometimes, fonts at small sizes (notably script fonts) become very hard to read. Changing the Anti-alias setting to strong may help, but if it's still not enough, another option is to create a clone of the text block (Ctrl/Command+Shift+C). This clone appears in exactly the same location as the original text and has the effect of making the text bolder, because the anti-aliasing is in effect doubled.

You can use this technique in combination with a variety of Live Filters to create some pretty cool effects.

#54 Adding Text to a Path

When you design for a Web site, you always have to keep in mind that the Web works in straight lines and boxes. It's really a very linear, modular display medium. But designers always want to push beyond the conformity of a straight line to a box with rounded corners or a rough edge, or text that follows a curve. You create this kind of visual trickery with images. Even though the image is still a rectangle, the graphics within that box are not restricted in this way.

By exporting text as a graphic, you can get images of curved text or text that follows a zigzag pattern or even 90 degree turns. Typically, these kinds of images are used for logos and graphics that add some zing to a design but not for the main body of page text. This should be done sparingly because any text that is exported as a graphic is not indexed by search engines, nor is it any more accessible to the visually impaired than a regular graphic would be.

Adding text to a path in Fireworks is a three-step process:

1. Use the Pen tool or other vector tool to draw a path (See Chapter 4, "Staying on the (Vector) Path," for more on working with vectors).

2. Type the text.

3. Select both objects, and then choose Text > Attach to Path. It's as simple as that!

Once you have attached some text to a path, other options become active in the Text menu. You can change the orientation of the text—how it distorts as it follows the path—by selecting one of four options in the Orientation menu (**Figure 54a**):

- **Rotate Around Path (default).** Baseline of text follows path exactly, so on a curved path each character may be angled in a different direction.

- **Vertical.** Text remains vertical and follows path.

- **Skew Vertical.** Distorts text vertically so that the baseline of text follows a path, but the text remains vertical.

- **Skew Horizontal.** Width of text is distorted as it follows a path. You can create a slight 3-D look because the text appears to be twisting.

Controlling Text Direction and Starting Point

You can also change the direction of your text. The initial direction of text is set by the direction in which you create the path. If you draw your path from right to left, the text will appear upside down and backwards when attached to a path. Select Text > Reverse Direction to run the text in the opposite direction. If you want your text to start at a point on the path other than the starting point, use the Text Offset field in the Property Inspector. This field is only visible when you have text attached to a path.

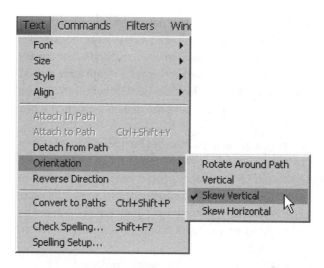

Figure 54a Options for controlling how the text conforms to the path are found in the Text menu.

Even though the two objects are merged, you edit the text and the path separately. Use the Text tool in conjunction with the Property Inspector to select and edit the text. Use the Subselection tool to edit the path shape or length (**Figure 54b**) and the Pen tool to add additional control handles to the path.

Figure 54b If you find that the end of your text disappears when it is attached to a path, use the Subselection tool to make the path longer.

#55 Wrapping Text Around an Object

For a long time Fireworks designers have wanted the ability to make text flow around an object, usually to emulate how text wraps around a floated image on a Web page. Prior to CS4, you could only mock this up by using a series of separate text boxes and placing them around the image.

CS4 has a new command called Attach In Path, which allows text to flow within any vector shape. It's still a mock-up, but it's much faster and more flexible than working with multiple text boxes.

Let's use the example of faking a CSS floated image.

Figure 55a shows an image and a rectangular block of text. Let's say you want the text to flow around the image, top and bottom.

Lorem ipsum dolor sit amet, consectetuer adipiscing elit, sed diam nonummy nibh euismod tincidunt ut laoreet dolore magna aliquam erat volutpat. Ut wisi enim ad minim veniam, quis nostrud exerci tation ullamcorper suscipit lobortis nisl ut aliquip ex ea commodo consequat. Duis autem vel eum iriure dolor in hendrerit in vulputate velit esse molestie consequat, vel illum dolore eu feugiat nulla facilisis at vero eros et accumsan et iusto odio dignissim qui blandit praesent luptatum zzril delenit augue duis dolore te feugait nulla facilisi.

Lorem ipsum dolor sit amet, consectetuer adipiscing elit, sed diam nonummy nibh euismod tincidunt ut laoreet dolore magna aliquam erat volutpat. Ut wisi enim ad minim veniam, quis nostrud exerci tation ullamcorper suscipit lobortis nisl ut aliquip ex ea commodo consequat. Duis autem vel eum iriure dolor in hendrerit in vulputate velit esse molestie consequat, vel illum dolore eu feugiat nulla facilisis at vero eros et accumsan et iusto odio dignissim qui blandit praesent luptatum zzril delenit augue duis dolore te feugait nulla facilisi.

Lorem ipsum dolor sit amet, consectetuer adipiscing elit, sed diam nonummy nibh euismod tincidunt ut laoreet dolore magna aliquam erat volutpat. Ut wisi enim ad minim veniam, quis nostrud exerci tation ullamcorper suscipit lobortis nisl ut aliquip ex ea commodo consequat. Duis autem vel eum iriure dolor in hendrerit in vulputate velit esse molestie consequat, vel illum dolore eu feugiat nulla facilisis at vero eros et accumsan et iusto odio dignissim qui blandit praesent luptatum zzril delenit augue duis dolore te feugait nulla facilisi.

Figure 55a The text needs to wrap around the image on the right.

1. Draw a rectangle that covers the text and the photo area. Hide this rectangle by clicking the eye icon in the Layers panel.

2. Draw a second rectangle that is slightly larger than the image. You might want to change the color of this shape so it is easier to see what you're doing.

3. Make the large rectangle visible again. Select both rectangles by Shift-clicking on each. You should see light blue control handles around each shape (**Figure 55b**).

(continued on next page)

Figure 55b Both rectangles are selected.

4. Open the Path panel. If you can't find it, select Window > Others > Path.

5. Choose Punch from the Combine Paths row (**Figure 55c**).

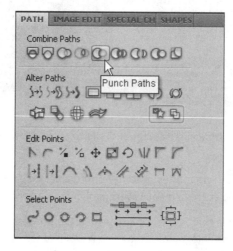

Figure 55c The Path panel is a quick way to perform many operations on vector tools, including punching a hole through a shape.

This operation uses the uppermost of the two rectangles to punch a hole in the rectangle below it. You should now see your photo peeking though the new opening, as shown in **Figure 55d**.

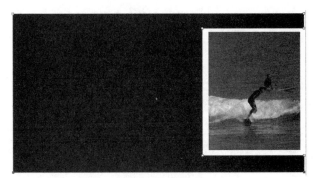

Figure 55d The successfully completed punch.

Tip
If you hold down the Shift key while selecting control handles, you can move more than one handle at the same time. This is great for keeping your shape squared up.

6. From the Layers panel, select the punched rectangle and the text. Then choose Text > Attach in Path. The text now flows within the custom shape (**Figure 55e**).

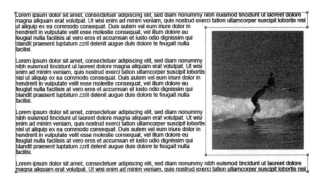

Figure 55e Text flows within the custom vector shape and remains editable.

Inserting Placement Text for Mock-ups

There will be times when you need to add text to a design, even if you don't have the actual copy but still need to show how text will interact with graphics or a Web page design. This is where Lorem Ipsum text can come in quite handy and—wouldn't you know it—Fireworks has a built-in command to generate this nonsense text.

You do not need to select the Text tool first. Just choose Commands > Text > Lorem Ipsum. Fireworks loads a single paragraph of text into a text area.

You can adjust the attributes of this text just like you can with text you type or import.

You can still edit the text with the Text tool or use the Subselection tool to alter the path shape. If you change the shape or size of the path, the text will reflow to match the new settings, as shown in **Figure 55f**.

Figure 55f An example of how text would reflow if the path is reshaped.

If the design in the figure is indeed a mock-up for a Web page, chances are good you would not try to display text following an angle because Web browsers like content in rectangular packages. You don't have to worry about shape limitations if you plan to convert the text to a graphic.

#56 Setting Text Anti-aliasing

Smoothing out the edges of text is referred to as anti-aliasing. Text anti-aliasing controls how the edges of the text blend into the background so that large text is cleaner, more readable, and more pleasing to the eye. This is accomplished by examining the color values of the edges of objects and the background that they are on, and blending the pixels at the edges based on the Anti-Alias settings.

By default, text has Smooth anti-aliasing applied to it. Small font sizes tend to be easier to read when anti-aliasing is removed.

Anti-aliasing applies to all characters in a given text block.

Once you have some text in place, you can adjust how it will display using the Property Inspector.

Why would you change text aliasing? Text on a Web page is displayed as aliased text—crisp with no blended edges. If the text in your design is supposed to look like true HTML text, you may want to set the text to No Anti-Alias in the Property Inspector.

To change text aliasing, open the Property Inspector and select from one of four preset alias settings or a custom setting (**Figure 56**) in the Anti-Alias pop-up menu:

Figure 56 The Anti-Alias settings are located in their own drop-down menu in the Property Inspector.

- **No Anti-Alias.** Disables text smoothing completely. Text is not blended and anything but horizontal or vertical lines are noticeably jagged. While not ideal for large text, it can actually make text at small sizes (8 point or less) easier to read.

- **Crisp Anti-Alias.** Displays a hard transition between the edges of the text and the background. Some blending occurs, but text still appears sharp.

- **Strong Anti-Alias.** Creates an abrupt transition between the text edges and the background, preserving the shapes of the text characters and

(continued on next page)

enhancing detailed areas of the characters. Text almost appears bold in comparison to Crisp Anti-Alias.

- **Smooth Anti-Alias.** Creates a soft blend between the edges of the text and the background, and is the default for text pasted into Fireworks.

- **Custom Anti-Alias.** When Custom Anti-Alias is selected, you can choose from these options in the pop-up menu that appears:

  - **Oversampling.** Sets the amount of detail used for creating the transition between the text edges and the background.

  - **Sharpness.** Sets the smoothness of the transition between the text edges and the background.

  - **Strength.** Sets how much the text edges blend into the background.

CHAPTER EIGHT

Exploring Creative Options

The preceding chapters covered many Fireworks basics. Now you will begin to dig a little deeper (and have a bit of fun too) by exploring some of the more advanced features within Fireworks. In this chapter you'll learn about the special effects options that come with Fireworks and about a couple of time-saving commands.

#57 Creating Movement with Blur Filters

The Filters Menu

The main Filters menu contains several submenus that include a number of commands:

- **Adjust Color.** Auto Levels, Brightness/ Contrast, Curves, Hue/ Saturation, Invert, and Levels

- **Blur.** Blur, Blur More, Gaussian Blur, Motion Blur, Radial Blur, and Zoom Blur

- **Noise.** Add Noise

- **Other.** Convert to Alpha and Find Edges

- **Sharpen.** Sharpen, Sharpen More, and Unsharp Mask

The Filters menu contains a solid set of special effect and image correction commands, such as Levels, Auto Levels, Gaussian Blur, and Unsharp Mask. The differences between Standard Filters and Live Filters were discussed in Technique #25 in Chapter 3, "Working with Bitmap Images." Filters applied from this menu can only be applied to bitmap objects. If you try to apply one of these Standard Filters to a vector object, Fireworks will warn you that the object must first be flattened and converted to a bitmap. Generally, most designers won't want to flatten vectors just to apply an effect, so skip to Technique #58 to see how you can have the best of both worlds.

Discussing each filter in the Filters menu is beyond the scope of this book, but let's look at how to create a sense of movement using some Blur filters and bitmap selections. This will give you the hang of things and allow you to see the potential of using filters. As always, continued experimentation will benefit you greatly.

Figure 57a shows a couple of cyclists enjoying the Pacific Coast Highway. To create a real sense of speed, you can use a combination of the Zoom Blur and Motion Blur filters. But first be sure to create a clone of the image to work on.

Figure 57a The original photo doesn't really give a sense of movement.

1. Choose the Lasso tool and draw a rough selection over the back half of the nearest cyclist. Include some of the background roadway as well. The final selection should look something like **Figure 57b**.

Figure 57b Filter effects are isolated to a bitmap selection, when one is present.

2. In the Property Inspector, change the edge of the Live Marquee to Feather and set the value to 10. Feathering gives you a selection that blends pixels inside and outside the marquee for a smooth transition.

Tip

Check out Chapter 3 for more details on making and editing bitmap selections.

3. Press Ctrl/Command+H to hide the marquee edge or select View > Edges.

4. Select Filters > Blur > Zoom Blur, set the Amount to 15, and set the Quality to 100 in the dialog. Click OK (**Figure 57c**).

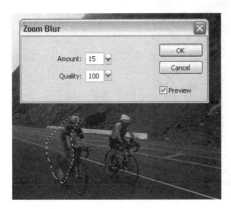

Figure 57c The Zoom Blur dialog gives you control over the amount (effect) and the quality (smoothness) of the blur.

(continued on next page)

5. Select Filters > Blur > Motion Blur, set the Angle to 160, and set the Distance to 5, as shown in **Figure 57d**.

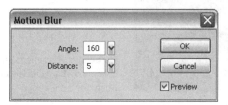

Figure 57d The Angle amount controls the direction of the Motion Blur.

The end result (shown with the original in **Figure 57e**) is pretty good. The Zoom Blur put the pixels in slightly different areas, emulating movement of the cyclist. The Motion Blur took those same pixels and blended them in a specific direction, similar to the effect a camera's slow shutter speed would have on a moving object. The Feathering ensured that the effect did not have a hard edge around it.

Figure 57e The before and after images for comparison.

#58 Live Filters for Ultimate Flexibility

You can apply Live Filters to bitmaps, vectors, groups, or even symbols without the risk of converting the object(s) to flattened bitmaps. That's cool point #1. Cool point #2 is that these filters are *always editable*. As long as the file has been saved as a Fireworks PNG, the filters won't permanently change the pixels they affect. As noted in Chapter 3, however, you cannot apply Live Filters to bitmap selections.

Live Filters are found in the Filters section of the Property Inspector. Just click the plus sign to launch the flyout menu (**Figure 58a**). Note that the Live Filters section contains many of the same categories as the Filters menu, plus several more, such as Shadow and Glow, Bevel and Emboss, and Photoshop Live Effects.

Live Filters and Symbols

If you convert multiple objects to a symbol, you can apply Live Filters to both the instance on the canvas and the individual objects within the symbol. You'll find more on symbols in Chapter 9 "Working with Symbols."

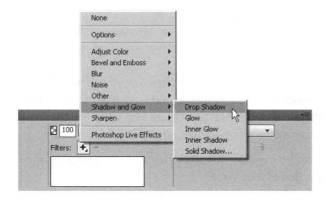

Figure 58a Multiple Live Filters can be found within each category.

Tip
Some Live Filters, such as Auto Levels and Find Edges, have no editable properties. In cases like this, the i icon will be grayed out.

The Shadow and Glow and Bevel and Emboss categories are great for adding depth to vector objects, giving them a bit more realism, as you will see shortly:

1. Draw an elliptical vector shape on the canvas and fill it with a solid color.

2. Click the plus sign and choose Shadow and Glow > Drop Shadow. Accept the default settings by pressing Enter/Return.

(continued on next page)

Live Filter Controls

Live Filters can also be *stacked* on an object. For example, you could use Auto Levels to improve the tonal range of an image, then apply Hue/Saturation to colorize the image, and then apply Noise to give the image the look of being shot with high-speed film.

Each applied filter will display in the Live Filters list box in the Property Inspector. You can change the stacking order of the filters to alter the overall effect, and you can also click the *i* icon to edit many of the filter's currently applied properties.

You can also toggle any Live Filter on or off without removing it from the list by clicking the check mark beside the filter name. And if you're sure you don't want the filter anymore, select the filter and click the minus sign just above the filter list to remove it.

3. Add an Inner Shadow effect by clicking the plus sign again and choosing Shadow and Glow > Inner Shadow. Set the Softness to a value of 2 instead of 4 and set the Angle to 114.

The shape now has a sense of depth because of the shadow.

4. To complete the effect, click the plus sign one more time and choose Shadow and Glow > Inner Shadow. Instead of accepting the defaults, change the color of the shadow to white, set the Softness to 2, and set the Angle to 298 (**Figure 58b**).

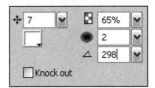

Figure 58b Adjusting the settings for the Inner Shadow.

5. Take a close look at the final shape, and then use your mouse to move the Drop Shadow filter to the bottom of the stack by click and dragging the filter within the combo box (**Figure 58c**). When you see a bold line display beneath the bottom filter, let go of the mouse button.

Note that placing the shadow in a different part of the stacking order changes the look of your shape.

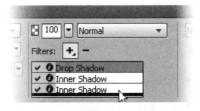

Figure 58c By changing the stacking order of the Live Filters, you can alter how they affect the object they are applied to.

#59 Using Photoshop Live Effects

Photoshop Live Effects are an interesting off-shoot of the integration between Fireworks and Photoshop. Photoshop has a range of editable effects called *Layer Styles*. In CS3 and CS4, Fireworks maintains the Photoshop Layer Styles and even provides the ability to make some basic changes to them by using the Photoshop Live Effects category of the Live Filters.

This can be a real time-saver if you need to work with Photoshop PSD files in Fireworks or have to export Fireworks designs as PSDs for other Photoshop users to work on.

While the effect options are not nearly as robust in Fireworks as they are in Photoshop, it does mean you can resave the file as a PSD file and those effects will remain editable in both Photoshop and Fireworks (**Figure 59a**).

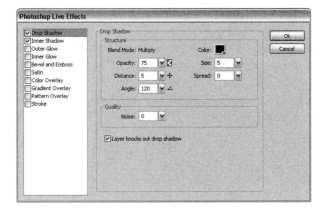

Figure 59a All the Photoshop Live Effects are handled through the same dialog, but you can only have one iteration of the Photoshop Live Filters applied to a given object. However, in that one iteration, you can apply one filter or all of the filters at the same time.

One Photoshop Live Effect that I quite like is the Stroke effect. Fireworks simply never had an equivalent to this for bitmaps. The Stroke effect adds a border around the visible pixels of any bitmap. **Figure 59b** shows a photo that has been masked and stroked. Click the plus sign, choose

Photoshop Live Effects

- Drop Shadow
- Inner Shadow
- Outer Glow
- Inner Glow
- Bevel and Emboss
- Satin
- Color Overlay
- Gradient Overlay
- Pattern Overlay
- Stroke

Fireworks Live Filters vs Photoshop Live Effects

Fireworks' native Live Filters are object-based, meaning they are applied just to the object regardless of the size of the canvas. Each filter has its own spot in the Applied Filters list. Photoshop Live Effects are applied via one large dialog and only occupy one spot on the Applied Filters list. After you have applied a Photoshop effect, you need to relaunch the Photoshop Live Effects dialog to add or edit other Photoshop Live Effects.

Figure 59b Using a mask in combination with a bitmap image gives you the ability to create a stroke around an image without having to create a custom vector shape.

Photoshop Live Effects, and then select the check box for Stroke. By default, a red 3-pixel border will follow the contour of the mask. You can also adjust other properties such as the opacity and position of the stroke. You can use vector or bitmap masks, and as you alter the mask, the stroke will change to follow the new shape.

#60 Working with Styles

Styles are prebuilt combinations of fills, Live Filters, strokes, and textures. Styles are a great jumping off point for getting the creative juices flowing. And applying them is easy! Styles are designed to work with vectors or type, but many of them have interesting effects on bitmap images as well.

The Styles panel lets you load in any of several preset style families, or you can browse for styles you might have downloaded from the Web (**Figure 60a**).

Figure 60a The Styles panel has been upgraded and updated for Fireworks CS4, making it easier to use.

Once you start applying styles to an object, they become part of the Current Document section of the Styles panel, making it easy for you to find the styles you've been trying out.

Often, you can have several objects with the same style—a set of navigation buttons or tabs for example. When you apply the same style to a series of objects (or just clone an object that has a style applied to it), each object is linked to the style. This comes in handy when you edit the properties of the style.

Try this:

1. Draw a rectangle.

2. Go to the Styles panel and load a style family. Then, with the rectangle still active, click on one of the styles.

3. Hold down the Alt/Option key and drag the shape with the Pointer tool to create a duplicate of the rectangle.

(continued on next page)

Applying Styles to Bitmaps

For more information on applying styles to bitmap images, check out my article "A Different Kind of Style" on Community MX at www.communitymx.com/content/article.cfm?cid=8D787.

Clearing Unused Styles

If you experiment with a lot of styles, the Current Document section can get overcrowded. To clear it of all unused styles, click the Options icon and choose Select Unused Styles. Then just click the trashcan icon at the bottom of the Styles panel to remove them from the list. The styles are just removed from the list, they are not deleted.

Exporting and Importing Styles

If you are working with a team, you can export your styles and send them to whoever needs them. Make sure nothing is selected on

(continued on next page)

the canvas or the first style you select will be applied to the active objects in your design. Select the style(s) you want to export, and then choose Save Style Library from the Styles panel Options. A Save dialog appears pointing to the Styles folder. Name the file, ending with .stl.

After the file is saved, you can attach it to an email and send it. The saved library also becomes one of your Style families.

To bring the styles into Fireworks, click the Options icon and choose Import Style Library. Browse to where the styles have been saved, select the .stl file, and click Open. The styles will be added to the Styles folder and be made available to any file, just by selecting the Style name from the Styles panel drop-down list.

Selecting and Saving Multiple Styles

To select and save multiple styles, hold down the Ctrl/ Command key and click on each style you want to save. Then choose New Style from the Options menu.

4. Repeat step 3.

5. With any one of the three shapes active, make some changes to the style using the Properties Inspector, even if it's just the fill color.

Now look at the Property Inspector. At the right side you'll see some options for styles. The current Style name will appear in the drop-down menu, and if you changed the style, you will see a plus sign beside the name.

Below the style name are several icons. The second one from the left is the Redefine Style icon. Click this icon and any objects that have the affected style will be updated (**Figure 60b**). If you like what you've created, you can name it and save it.

Figure 60b Updating linked styles, creating new ones, and even breaking the link between objects with the same style can all be handled through the Property Inspector.

Make sure one of the objects with the style is active to display the proper style thumbnail. Select the style in the Current Document section of the Styles panel. Click the Options icon (upper-right corner of the panel) and choose New Style. Name the style. You can turn off style attributes at this time as well, but chances are you'll want exactly what you see, so leave the attributes as they are and click OK (**Figure 60c**).

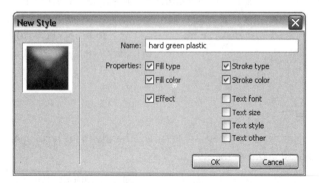

Figure 60c You are not limited to the styles that come with Fireworks. You can create your own new, custom styles as well.

#61 Using Blend Modes

Blend modes are unsung heroes in Fireworks. There are a total of 45 to play with. You can apply blend modes to layers *or* objects in Fireworks. The impact of a blend mode is controlled primarily by the colors in the images being blended but also by the opacity of the layer or object.

Blend modes affect how the colors of one layer or object blend with the colors of a layer or object directly below it. If you apply a blend mode from the Layers panel, it affects the entire layer or object.

Each object and each layer can have its own blend mode.

You can apply blend modes to vector tools such as the Shapes, Text, Pen, and Line tools. You can set the blend mode before you draw or afterwards. Blend modes applied to vector images are always editable, even if the vector is filled with a bitmap texture or pattern.

Another great feature of blend modes is that you can apply them with the bitmap Paint tools (Paint Brush, Pencil, and Paint Bucket). Select the tool, choose a fill color, choose a blend mode from the Property Inspector, and then paint. This technique gives you very detailed control over the effect of a blend mode, but unlike object and layer application, this method is also destructive, changing pixels permanently. This feature may be very useful to those with drawing tablets.

Every blend mode available can't be examined in this book. However, let's explore a technique for improving the image quality in a photograph.

If you have an image that is over exposed (too bright), you can use the Multiply blend mode to visually improve the exposure. Start by creating a clone of the image. Then, in the Layers panel, select the uppermost of the two images and set the Blend Mode to Multiply (**Figure 61a**).

Blend Mode Categories

Blend modes are divided into ten different categories in Fireworks. This is how I classify them:

- **Opacity modes.** Normal and Average and Dissolve

- **Darken modes.** Darken, Multiply, Color Burn, Inverse Color Burn, Soft Burn, and Linear Burn

- **Lighten modes.** Lighten, Screen, Color Dodge, Inverse Color Dodge Soft, and Linear Dodge

- **Lighting effects modes.** Overlay, Soft Light, Fuzzy Light, Hard Light, Vivid Light, Linear Light, Pin Light, and Hard Mix

- **Invert modes.** Difference, Exclusion, and Negation

- **Color modes.** Hue, Saturation, Color, Luminosity, Red, Green, and Blue

(*continued on next page*)

- **Thermal modes.** Reflect, Glow, Heat, and Freeze (OK, so Thermal is my idea, but with blend mode names like heat and freeze, I couldn't help myself.)

- **Math modes.** Additive, Subtractive, Subtract, Interpolation, Stamp, and XOR

- **Invert and Tint modes.** Are grouped together, but I think they'd be happier in the Invert and Color families

- **Erase mode.** Fills object with current canvas color

Blend Mode Elements

- **Opacity.** The degree of transparency to which the blend mode is applied

- **Blend color.** The color you add with your Paint tool or that is already on the layer that has the blend mode applied

- **Base color.** The color of pixels under the blend color

- **Result color.** The effect after blending

Figure 61a Blend modes work by blending the colors of one image with images below it, so make sure you apply your blend mode to an image that is above another object. You can check this in the Layers panel.

If left at 100% Opacity, Multiply effectively doubles the exposure, adding density to the highlights, midtones, and shadows. If the effect is too strong, try reducing the opacity of the object with the mode. The results can be pretty significant, as shown in **Figure 61b**.

Figure 61b The image on the left is the original file, which is slightly overexposed and suffering from haze created by the surf. The image on the right has two identical objects, the top one was blended using Multiply.

Photoshop Compatible Modes

Many Fireworks' blend modes are compatible with Photoshop, including the seven most common ones in Photoshop:

- Dissolve
- Linear Burn
- Linear Dodge
- Vivid Light
- Linear Light
- Pin Light
- Hard Mix

If the same Fireworks blend mode exists in Photoshop, Photoshop will recognize the mode if you open an exported PSD version of your Fireworks file.

Flash Compatible Blend Modes

Flash also supports many of the Fireworks blend modes! When Flash reads the data in an unflattened Fireworks PNG file, the supported blend modes are understood and converted to the corresponding blend modes in Flash:

- Darken
- Multiply
- Lighten
- Screen
- Overlay
- Hard light
- Add
- Subtract
- Difference
- Invert
- Erase

Blend Mode Math

Frankly, I never realized how much math was involved in blend modes. I don't pretend to understand the formulas, but if you are interested, be sure to check out www.pegtop.net/delphi/articles/blendmodes for more algebra than you can shake a PNG file at.

Brightening a Dark Image

If you have an image that is too dark, you can use the Screen, Linear Dodge, or Additive blend mode in much the same manner as described with the Multiply blend mode to lighten the image. Screen mode is the most subtle of the three modes, Linear Dodge and Additive have more of an impact on image contrast, so you may want to experiment with object opacity.

#62 Converting Bitmap Selections to Paths

This technique and #63 can be quite useful for applying masks, converting bitmap images to vectors, or softening corners on a sharp vector shape without resorting to the Pen tool. And they are fast to apply, once you have created your selection or path.

Sometimes it can be quicker to create a bitmap selection using the Magic Wand tool than it would be to use the Pen tool to draw a path. But what if you need the selection in a vector form? For example, say you've been supplied with a client's logo, but it's only in bitmap form. You need to make alterations to the logo—resize it, change colors, and so on—but these changes can have undesirable results because you would be altering the pixels of the image. A vector format, however, can be scaled, colored, and even filled with another image without damaging the object. You can convert a bitmap selection in Fireworks to a vector path easily.

You first create the selection. If you only want the shape of the image, use the Magic Wand to select the area outside the image, assuming it's a solid color (the Magic Wand is great for quickly selecting areas of solid color). Choose Select > Select Inverse to place the selection around the actual image. Then choose Select > Convert Marquee to Path (**Figure 62a**).

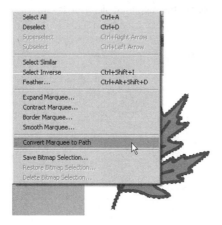

Figure 62a Converting a bitmap selection to a path is a very simple process.

Instantly, you will have a vector object that matches the previous selection. You can then scale, stroke, or color it as desired (**Figure 62b**).

Figure 62b Compare the original bitmap object (right) with the vector version. Additional strokes using the Vector Path tool were added to mimic the veining in the leaf.

#63 Converting Paths to Bitmap Selections

Don't Lose Your Path!

Converting a path to a marquee deletes the selected path by default. You can change this setting by selecting Edit > Preferences > Edit (Adobe Fireworks > Preferences > Edit), and then deselecting the check box for Delete paths when converting to marquee. This way, you will always have the original vector available.

Create a Bitmap Selection Using the Layers Panel

You can also create a bitmap selection by selecting a bitmap object in the Layers panel, and then holding down the Alt/Option key and clicking on the vector shape object. If you do not have any bitmap objects in the file, create an empty bitmap object by clicking the New Bitmap Image icon in the Layers panel. It's just to the left of the trashcan icon.

This trick also works with bitmaps. Alt/Option-clicking on a bitmap object will create a marquee around the perimeter of the bitmap

If you need to create a selection around a complex bitmap or one without a uniform background color, using the Pen tool may be faster (and definitely more controllable) than using the Lasso or Polygon Lasso tool. Once a path is created it's a snap to convert it to a bitmap selection so that you can edit it with any of the bitmap tools.

If you are creating a custom path, use the Pen tool to add the path around the area. Refer back to Technique #36 in Chapter 4, "Staying on the (Vector) Path," for more information on the Pen tool.

After the path is created, you can use the Subselection tool to tweak its shape (**Figure 63a**). When you are satisfied, select Modify > Convert Path to Marquee. Set your marquee edge to Hard, Anti-alias, or Feather and click OK.

Figure 63a Vectors can be more accurate than bitmap selections because the path is not based on selecting pixels.

You can use this selection for a bitmap mask or apply bitmap treatments to it, as shown in **Figure 63b**.

Figure 63b The marquee was feathered and then used as a bitmap mask to hide the surrounding pixel detail.

CHAPTER NINE

Working with Symbols

Symbols are one of the great time-saving features in Fireworks, and they've been around since the beginning of the application. Symbols are a way to contain multiple objects within a single asset but still have quick access to editing those objects. They come in very handy if you are using an object over and over again—for example, a navigation button or a logo. Symbols can contain a single object, or they can contain text, vectors, and bitmaps, each with their own Live Filter attributes.

A symbol is a master version of a graphic. When you place a symbol on the canvas, you're actually placing a copy of the symbol, which is known as an *instance*.

Symbols are much more than a collection of reusable objects. You can build your own as you will see, but Fireworks also comes with a wealth of predesigned symbol objects that you can use as part of your designs or as a starting point for jump-starting your own creative talents.

When you edit the original *symbol object*, the linked *instances* on the canvas automatically change to reflect the edited symbol.

Three main types of symbols are available within Fireworks: graphic, button, and animation symbols. There is also an enhanced graphic symbol type referred to as *component symbols*. You'll look at each of these in the following techniques.

#64 Creating Graphic Symbols

Graphic symbols are static objects, meaning they don't have any built-in animation or interactivity. I use graphic symbols for common elements like logos or if I have a higher-resolution photo that I may need to use in various parts of my design at different lower resolutions (see the sidebar, "Resizing Symbols").

To make a graphic symbol, select the object (or objects) using the Pointer tool. Then either press F8/Command+F8 or select Modify > Symbol > Convert to Symbol. From the dialog that appears (**Figure 64a**) you can name the symbol (recommended), choose the type of symbol, and enable options such as 9-Slice Scaling Guides and whether the symbol becomes part of the Common Library.

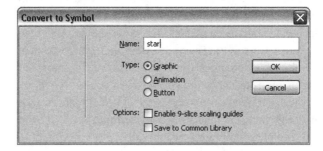

Figure 64a The Convert to Symbol dialog is control central for creating new symbols.

By default, symbols are saved *with* the currently active document. Open a new file and you won't be able to find that new symbol in the Document Library unless you first export the symbol from the original document and then *import* it into the current document. The other option is to use the Save to Common Library option, which allows the symbol to be used in multiple documents (see the sidebar, "Where Did My Symbol Go?").

Choose Graphic from the Type list, leave the options deselected, and click OK. On the canvas you should now see a copy—or instance—of the newly created symbol. When selected, you'll see a small blue cross in the middle of the instance (**Figure 64b**). This is your symbol indicator. If your symbol was originally a single bitmap, that's about the only difference you will notice. If your object was a vector, you'll notice that the vector control handles and vector path are not visible.

Resizing Symbols

When you resize any bitmap to a smaller size, pixel information is discarded. This is normally a permanent change to the file, and the only way to regain the data is to import or open the original larger file again. Vectors do not have this problem; however, a bitmap fill (pattern) may suffer from quality loss.

If you convert a high-resolution bitmap image to a symbol, you can scale the instance of the symbol as often you want without damaging the original symbol. The secret is to make sure you only scale the image to sizes smaller than the original. If you try to make the instance larger in dimension than the master symbol, the image quality will suffer.

Figure 64b An instance is designated by the faint cross in the middle of an object.

Note
The small blue cross also acts as a registration point to help you align text or other objects to the center of the symbol.

Navigating Through Symbols

While in symbol editing mode, you will also see bread crumb navigation at the top of the document, indicating which symbol is being edited and how deep you have *drilled down* into the symbol. This ties in with another new feature of Fireworks: nested symbols. For an added degree of control, you can nest symbols within each other, keeping your entire design element for an object within one main symbol. More on nested symbols in the sidebar on page 146.

This bread crumb structure temporarily replaces the preview views above the canvas area. You can click on the various bread crumbs markers to return to the original page or to any other marker visible in the trail. (Bread crumb trails for symbols are found in Flash as well—part of the unified workspace efforts that Adobe is using to tie their products together.)

Where Did My Symbol Go?

When creating a new symbol, saving it to the Common Library will remove the object from the canvas. You will need to locate the newly created symbol in the Common Library panel and insert it back into your document.

The advantage to enabling the Save to Common Library option in the Convert to Symbol dialog is that the new symbol becomes available to *any* document you work on, not just the current document. More on this in Technique #69.

#65 Creating Button Symbols

The Button symbol is a symbol with a very specific purpose: making button rollover states.

Draw the shape you want to use for the button. Typically, buttons are a derivative of a rectangle. Add Live Filters, fills, and strokes as you see fit.

With the size of the button and the text decided (see the sidebar, "The Name Game"), add the text to the button by typing with the Text tool. Set your text alignment to center alignment in the Property Inspector to keep the text centered regardless of its length.

Use the Pointer tool in conjunction with Smart Guides to position the text in the exact horizontal and vertical center of the shape. Select both objects and press F8/Command+F8. Name the symbol (call it button or some other logical name) and this time choose Button as the Type. Leave the options deselected (you'll get to them, don't worry) and click OK.

This time Fireworks adds a slice around the instance. Buttons are generally interactive and use more than one state. Fireworks assumes (and rightly so) that an object-based slice will be needed.

For now, hide the slice by selecting the Hide slices and hotspot icon in the Tools panel. Double-click the button instance to get to symbol editing mode. The Property Inspector changes to reflect options for the button symbol (**Figure 65a**).

Figure 65a Button symbols have special interactive properties not found in graphic symbols.

Most notably, you now have a pop-up menu listing all the possible button states and the Active Area for the button, as shown in **Figure 65b**.

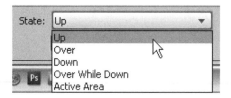

Figure 65b A button symbol can have up to four distinct visual states.

What's So Cool About Button Symbols?

Button symbols are a very efficient way to generate up to four visible states for a button (Up, Over, Down, and Over While Down) and add a hyperlink to them. Almost any graphic or text object can become a button. After you have created a single button symbol, you can reuse it again and again for navigation. Each instance of a button symbol can also have its own custom text, URL, and target without breaking the symbol-instance relationship.

A button instance is self-contained. All the graphic elements and states are kept together, so as you move the Up state of a button on the canvas, the other states and the button slice move with it.

When you export a button, Fireworks can generate the JavaScript necessary to display it in a Web browser. In Adobe Dreamweaver, you can easily insert JavaScript and HTML code from Fireworks into your Web pages or into any HTML file (very handy for interactive HTML prototypes). For production sites, most designers opt to create the code and JavaScript by hand or from within Dreamweaver.

Choose the Over state. (This is where you determine how the button will appear when the cursor is placed *over* the image.) Your button disappears from the canvas, because as yet you don't have anything created for that state. This is easy enough to fix: Click the Copy Up Graphic button. A copy of your original button appears. Make some changes to the button in this state—perhaps add a glow around the text or change the button or text color. If you toggle between the Up and Over states, you'll see the beginnings of a simple rollover. Most rollovers use just these two basic states, but you can add Down and Over While Down states if you think you will need them.

Creating additional buttons from the same symbol is easy and can be done in many ways, but as long as one instance is on the canvas, Alt/Option dragging is the fastest method. Select the button instance. Hold down the Alt/Option key and click and drag the button. You get an instant copy that is still linked to the main symbol. And with Smart Guides active, Fireworks even helps you line up things nice and neat. The cool thing here is the button text: In the Property Inspector is a text input field and whatever you type into that box is what the new button's text becomes.

Tip
You can also import one of several prebuilt button symbols by clicking the Import button in the Property Inspector. See the Fireworks Help files for more information on importing buttons.

What Is the Active Area?
The Active Area is the automatic slice created by Fireworks. You can select that option and manually edit the size of the slice using either the Pointer tool or the Scale tool.

CSS Rollovers
Many Web designers now use background images and CSS to create a button rollover effect, but button symbols can't be beat for creating interactive HTML prototypes or for creating the background images for CSS-based rollovers.

The Name Game
Before you make your button symbol, take the time to determine the longest button name. This will help you establish a consistent size for the text so you don't create button text at different font sizes just so the names fit within the button dimensions.

LIve Filters and the Active Area
If you added any kind of outer glow or drop shadow, the slice may be noticeably larger than the button. This is Fireworks ensuring that the Live Filter effect is not cut off when it is sliced. To reduce the size of the slice, the best thing to do is reduce the size and softness of the filter.

#66 Creating Animation Symbols

Fireworks' Animation Potential

The animation capabilities in Fireworks are pretty basic and are suitable for creating simple GIF animations. If you are interested in creating complex animations for the Web, it would be a good idea for you to investigate Adobe Flash.

Like a button symbol, an animation symbol is self-contained. You can create an animation symbol from scratch or by converting an object to a symbol. You can then set properties that determine the number of states in the animation and the type of action (scaling, rotation, and opacity).

Because animations require additional frames not needed for most of a design, you should create animations in their own document or page.

Select or create the object you want to animate and press F8/Command+F8. Name the symbol and choose Animation Symbol. The Animate dialog appears (**Figure 66a**) with animation options. For any animation to occur, you must select a state value higher than 1. Because the end result of these animations is usually GIF animations, try to keep the state count low—the more states you have, the larger the final file size will be.

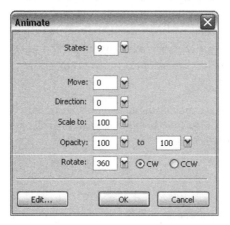

Figure 66a The Animate dialog let's you set various animation attributes. Smoother animations are created by adding more states, but this also increases file size.

Set your animation options and click OK. Fireworks will warn you that it needs to add additional states to the document. If you want the animation to work, you must click OK.

If you select the animation instance, the Property Inspector displays the same animation options as those in Figure 66a. Double-clicking the instance allows you to edit the physical characteristics of the object, such as fill, filters, stroke, and so on.

You can also add Live Filters to the individual instance, just as you can with other symbol types.

If your animation symbol includes movement across the canvas, you will see a path showing the distance and angle of the movement (**Figure 66b**).

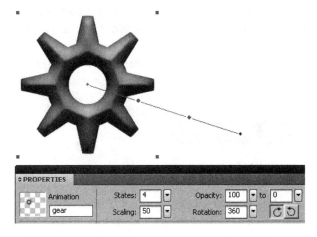

Figure 66b Each square along the path represents the location of the object in a specific state.

Testing and Exporting

You can test the animation by using the playback controls near the bottom right of the document window. To change the speed of the animation, open the States panel and change the State Delay value from the default of 7/100 of a second. Each state can have its own delay value. If you want the delay identical for each state, Shift-click to select all the states and then double-click on any delay value. Enter a new value (a lower number is faster) and press Enter/Return.

For the animation to run in a Web page, you must slice the instance and set the optimization to Animated GIF. On export, this will export all the states of the animation as a single, interleaved file.

#67 Editing Symbols

To edit an actual symbol, double-click anywhere on the instance to take advantage of *in-place symbol editing*. Everything but the selected symbol will appear slightly faded. You can also enter this mode by selecting Modify > Symbol > Edit in Place. If you have multiple instances of the same symbol on the canvas and you change the look of the symbol, in-place symbol editing (similar to Flash's symbol editing workflow) gives you an instant update to all instances. This can be very helpful if you are trying to customize the visual appearance of button shapes, graphic bullets, or the outline around containers for Web page content (often referred to as pods).

To exit symbol editing mode, double-click on the canvas or use the bread crumb trail above the canvas area (**Figure 67**; also see the sidebar, "Navigating Through Symbols").

Figure 67 The bread crumb trail shows you exactly how far you have drilled into a symbol.

Another option for editing symbols is referred to as *isolation mode*. This is the default mode for any symbol to which the 9-Slice Scaling Guides option has been applied. You can access isolation mode by selecting Modify > Symbol > Edit Symbol. The symbol remains on the canvas, but all other objects are hidden from view.

Once in symbol editing mode, you can select any object to edit its properties. Changes to the symbol will also be reflected in any instances on the canvas.

To edit only the current instance, break the link between the instance and the symbol by selecting Modify > Symbol > Break Apart. This permanently breaks the relationship between the selected instance and the symbol. Any future edits you make to the symbol won't be reflected in the former instance.

To exit symbol editing mode (in-place or isolation), simply double-click on canvas area not occupied by the symbol or click on the bread crumb marker.

Adjusting or locking 9-Slice Scaling Guides can only be performed on a symbol when you are in edit mode. Unlike the 9-Slice Transform tool, the placement of the scaling guides remains with the symbol and the scaling guides do not reset back to their defaults once you have scaled the instance.

#**68** Importing and Exporting Symbols

Symbols can be shared among users in much the same way as styles can be shared (Technique #60). Choose Export Symbols from the Document Library panel's Options menu. Select the symbols, press the Export button (**Figure 68**), and navigate to a folder. All selected symbols are saved as a single PNG file. Then it's just a matter of emailing the PNG file to the other members of your team.

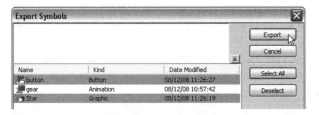

Figure 68 You can use the Shift key to select all the symbols or the Ctrl/Command key to make noncontiguous selections.

You have a few options for importing symbols: use the Import Symbols command in the Document Library Options menu, drag and drop an instance from one document to another, or copy and paste an instance. In all cases the symbol is made available only to the destination document.

When you drag and drop or copy and paste, the symbol maintains a link to the symbol from the original document.

Update Exported Symbols and Instances

Because imported symbols remain linked to their original symbol document, you can edit the original symbol document and then choose to update the target documents to reflect the edits.

1. In the original document, modify the symbol in symbol editing mode.
2. Save the file.
3. In the document where the symbol was imported, select the symbol in the Document Library panel.
4. Select Update from the Document Library panel Options menu.

#69 The Common Library

If you want your symbols to be available to new or existing documents, other than the current one, save them to the Common Library. This can be done while you are creating a new symbol, or you can select a symbol in the Document Library and choose Save to Common Library from the Options menu.

The Common Library is also full of prebuilt symbols that you can use in any document. The types of symbols include prebuilt animation symbols, graphic symbols, Web and application symbols, 2D objects, and button symbols, as well as navigation bars and Flex and HTML component symbols.

To add one of these symbols to the Common Library, open a Fireworks document, and then select a folder in the Common Library panel.

Choose the symbol you want to import into your document. You can drag and drop the symbol name or the preview on the canvas to insert it into your design (**Figure 69**). It also then becomes part of your Document Library.

Figure 69 Symbols from the Common or Document Libraries are added to the canvas by dragging and dropping.

Note
The Common Library does not become populated with symbols until a document is open in Fireworks.

#70 Adding Component Symbols to a Design

Adobe is positioning Fireworks as a tool for creating more than just Web page designs. It now has features that aid in the development of a wide variety of interface designs such as *programmable* component symbols, all of which are found in the Common Library panel. They can be intelligently scaled (using the 9-Slice Scaling Guides) and given specific attributes using JavaScript.

Many of these symbols are UI related (buttons, check boxes, text fields, etc.), and the Symbol Properties panel (by default, grouped with the Property Inspector) lets you edit the *state* of certain component symbols as well as attributes such as text size and color. For example, you can make a Submit button look as if it is being hovered over or clicked without having to edit the symbol directly, as you would with other symbol types.

You add component symbols to a design in the same manner as you add regular symbols: drag and drop. They are located in the Common Library in the Flex, HTML, Mac, and Win folders. After you have placed a component symbol on the canvas, it will be added to the Document Library for the current document. If you need additional copies of the symbol, drag and drop them from the Document Library. If you try dragging the same symbol from the Common Library again, Fireworks will display a warning message.

HTML Component Symbols

The HTML component symbols, such as form elements, headings 1 through 6, and link, are not just for static mock-ups. If you export your page as CSS and Images, these symbols will be exported as true HTML (<h1>, <a href="…">) and HTML form elements. Fireworks even wraps the form elements in a form tag!

#71 Editing a Component Symbol

To edit a component symbol, select it on the canvas and then make the Symbol Properties panel active. You will see the various attributes that can be changed. For example, with a text field symbol selected, you can alter the text label, text field type, text color, font family and size, and the state of the field (**Figure 71a**). To edit the default text label, just select the word text in the Value column and type in your new label. Other attributes (such as Font Family) are changed by clicking on a drop-down menu. When you make changes in the Symbol Properties panel, only the selected instance is affected.

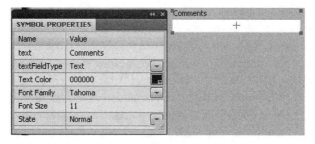

Figure 71a Each instance of a component symbol can be edited individually using the Symbol Properties panel.

Because these are symbols, you can also edit their physical appearance by double-clicking on the symbol. You can then edit the symbol as you would any other. Change the color, add a Live Filter, or use the 9-Slice Scaling Guides to ensure distortion-free transformations. Changes applied in symbol editing mode affect all instances linked to the symbol, just as with normal graphic symbols.

The text field symbol, as an example, looks like a single-line text entry box when it is first added to the canvas, but by placing 9-Slice Scaling Guides at the appropriate locations, you can safely scale a text field *instance* into a multiline comment box, as shown in **Figure 71b**. While editing the symbol, you can move the text label outside the field area; by default, this label is inside the field, but in most HTML forms you will see the label outside the field. This symbol has two states to choose from: *normal* and *selected*. While in symbol editing mode, you can change the properties of these states. For example, you might want the selected mode to show a specific background color inside the field. Simply choose the grouped object in the *selected* layer and change the background color in the Property Inspector. When you exit symbol editing mode, choose the Selected State in the Symbol Properties panel to see the color change.

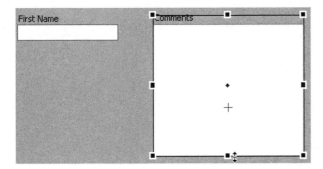

Figure 71b The Comments box is created by transforming a text field box.

CHAPTER TEN

Animation in Fireworks

As mentioned in Technique #66, if you are interested in creating complex animations for the Web, it would be a good idea for you to investigate Adobe Flash. That said, Fireworks does make it easy to build simple GIF animations and even export the animation as a SWF file. With the popularity of Flash and its ability to create rich interactive experiences, animated GIFs have taken a back seat in contemporary Web design, but they are still handy for quick, simple banner ads, animated progress bars, and the like.

#72 Creating GIF Animations

In Fireworks, animations are created using the States panel. Each state contains image elements that give your final animation some life. It can be as simple as a change in color. The bottom of the States panel (**Figure 72a**) has controls for the actual states, such as looping, onion skinning (seeing before and after states based on the currently selected state), adding/duplicating states, and distributing objects to states.

Onion Skinning   Distribute to States

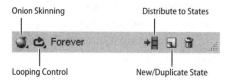

Looping Control   New/Duplicate State

Figure 72a Common state controls are found at the bottom of the States panel.

Try your hand at creating a simple, two-state animation:

1. Create a new document that is 200 px wide by 100 px high. Leave the background of your new document set to white. Make sure you can see your States panel and Layers panel.

2. In the Optimize panel set the Export File Format to Animated GIF.

3. Use the rectangle Shape tool from the Vector section of the toolbar and draw a shape on your canvas.

4. Use the Property Inspector to change the color of the shape to a shade of green.

5. Activate the States panel. You'll see only one state.

6. Add a duplicate by clicking the State Options icon (upper-right corner of States panel) and selecting Duplicate State. A new dialog appears (**Figure 72b**). You can leave everything at the default settings and click OK.

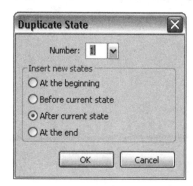

Figure 72b The Duplicate State dialog controls the number of duplicates to make and where they are inserted.

You now have two identical states.

What Is an Animated GIF?

GIF animation is an alternate version of the GIF file format, which allows for multiple images (or states) to be stacked inside a single file, and then played in sequence within a Web browser. If each state in the animation is slightly different, you get the appearance of movement or passage of time when these states are played in succession.

Animated GIFs can be set to play once or loop multiple or infinite times. State Delay can also be set, which can make the animation appear to run faster or slower.

A GIF animation is still only a single image as far as a Web browser is concerned; interactivity is limited to the entire image or the use of an image map. You can't set different hyperlinks on different states of the animation.

7. Select State 2, and then click on the green box in your document.

8. Use the Property Inspector to change the color to red and add a Red Glow Live Filter (Filters > Shadow and Glow > Glow in the Property Inspector).

9. Adjust the blur and displacement of the glow so it fits inside your canvas.

10. To preview the animation, use the animation controls at the bottom of the document window.

11. Save the file as a Fireworks PNG file for future editing.

12. Export the file (File > Export). Browse to a folder and save the file. You can load the file in a browser window to see it in action.

With this one simple animation you could do all sorts of things. If you click on State 2, for example, you could select the red box and move it to the right side of the canvas. Re-export and you get dancing boxes!

What Happened to Frames?

In previous versions of Fireworks, states were known as frames. The name switch was made to emphasize the use of the States panel for creating page compositions and interfaces rather than just animations.

Animation Speed

If you want your animation to move faster or slower, you need to adjust the State Delay timing in the States panel. The default for each State is 7/100s of a second (it just shows "7" in each state of the animation). You can double-click on the delay rate and change the value. A higher number forces each state to stay onscreen longer, hence slowing down the animation.

Creating an Animation Symbol

In Technique #66 you learned how to create an animation symbol from a single state object. You can turn a state-based animation into a symbol just as easily:

1. Click on State 1 to make it active, and then click on the Onion Skinning box for State 2 in the States panel.

2. Select all the objects by pressing Ctrl/Command+A.

3. Choose Modify > Symbol > Convert to Symbol, and then choose Animation.

4. Name your animation. Click OK.

5. The Animate dialog appears. Make sure that the number of frames is still set to 2. Leave everything else as is and click OK.

#73 Tweening Animation

Another way to create an animation is by using one or more instances of the same symbol in two different places on the canvas and *tweening* them. This method takes two instances of a symbol and fills in the changes be*tween* them to create an animation. *Tween* is an animation term for all the intermediate states of an animation sequence between the first and last states.

1. On the left side of the canvas, create a circle with the Vector tools and fill it with a color so it is easy to see.

2. Convert this object to a graphic symbol.

3. Hold down Alt/Option and drag the current instance to create a duplicate.

4. Move this duplicate to the right side of the canvas, and then Shift-click to select both instances.

5. Select Modify > Symbol > Tween Instances.

6. Make sure the Distribute to States option is selected, as shown in **Figure 73a**.

7. Set the number of states you think you will need. Keep in mind that this value will be added to the start and end states you already have on the canvas. Click OK.

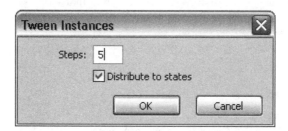

Figure 73a Tween Instances controls whether the tween occurs in a single layer or in multiple states.

At first you may think your second instance has disappeared, but if you open the States panel, you will see a whole new set of states. Click on each one to see where your circle is positioned. If you select the first state and

Gimme More!

Draw a shape. Any shape. Select Commands > Creative > Twist and Fade. When the dialog opens, be sure to select the Animate option, and then start playing. You can spend all day creating your own custom animations, but for a quick start, try out the presets found at the bottom left of the dialog. When you're satisfied, click OK and the command will automatically distribute each object to its own state. This command is a toy box in itself. One word of warning, though—keep the number of steps low-ish. Those steps all become states, which end up being frames in the final animated GIF.

If these techniques have whetted your appetite for GIF animations, feel free to check out some of my in-depth GIF animation tutorials at Community MX (http://tinyurl.com/6fwr4z).

then click on the Onion Skinning box for the last state, you will see each state's object in a semitransparent view, except for the selected state—it will appear totally opaque (**Figure 73b**).

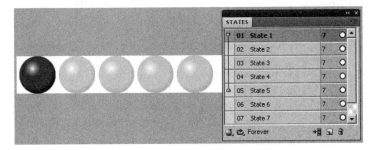

Figure 73b Onion skinning lets you see states that appear before and after the currently selected state.

Instance tweening gives you more control over the path of the animation than you get when you create a simple animation symbol, where movement can only travel in a straight line. With tweening, you can reposition each object within each state, creating a curved movement. After which you can always convert states to an animation symbol, as detailed in the sidebar "Creating an Animation Symbol" in Technique #72.

Plan Ahead

If you have an image that doesn't require animation, but you want it to appear in all the animation states, you can place it on its own layer and choose Share Layer to States from the Layer Options menu. Make sure the objects you want to animate are on a separate layer.

Planning your animation beforehand is a *very good* idea. Sharing a layer across states is best done *before you add any extra states*. If you add states first and then decide to share a layer, you run the risk of deleting any content that exists in that layer on other states.

#74 Shape Tweening

Yes you read that right. With the help of the Path panel and a command within the States Options, you can create a shape tween animation in Fireworks.

1. Start with a new document. Draw a circle and note its dimensions in the Property Inspector.

2. Draw another shape, perhaps a star. Change the fill color of the star and adjust its dimensions in the Property Inspector to match that of the circle.

3. Press Ctrl/Command+Shift+G to ungroup the star (certain shapes—such as auto shapes and the rectangle—need to be ungrouped before this technique will work). Align the two shapes so they are visibly centered over each other.

4. Select both shapes and open the Path panel (Window > Others > Path).

5. Click the Blend Paths icon in the Alter Paths section of the panel (**Figure 74a**). When the command dialog displays (**Figure 74b**), set the number of steps for the transformation. These steps will become states, so don't go overboard: Try to keep it to ten or less. Click OK.

Figure 74a The Path panel has some cool hidden gems.

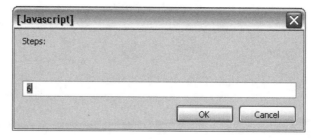

Figure 74b This dialog ultimately determines the number of states in the animation.

6. When the Flatten blended portions message displays (**Figure 74c**), click No.

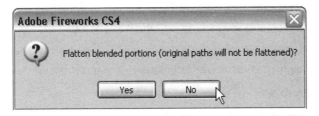

Figure 74c Don't flatten the blend or the animation effect will be lost.

7. Press Ctrl/Command+Shift+G twice to ungroup the shapes, because this Path command creates a nested group of all the shapes. If you look at the Layers panel, you should see that all the objects are selected. If they become deselected, just press Ctrl/Command+A to select them all again.

8. Choose Distribute to States from the State Options menu. If you press the play button at the bottom of the document window, you should see your animation transform in both shape and color.

#75 Optimizing and Exporting Animated GIFs

Index Transparency and Web Page Backgrounds

If you decide to use a transparent background for your GIF, Animated GIF, or PNG 8 files, make note of your Web page background color and use the Matte setting to eliminate edge artifacts.

Optimizing and exporting provide you with one more chance to squeeze out every last byte of data. What I like is that Fireworks gives you the chance to really *see* how your optimization decisions will affect the final image. There's no guess work here about results. Fireworks gives you many ways to optimize and export—and they're easy, too:

- **Optimize panel** (in conjunction with the 2-Up and 4-Up tab views, and the Export command; see Technique #47 for more details)
- **Image Preview** (File > Image Preview)
- **Export Wizard** (File > Export Wizard)

For a GIF animation, you get the most control by using the Image Preview dialog. This feature gives you a last minute chance to not only alter the color table, but also to change image dimensions, frame rate, transparency, and the disposal method of the background. The Image Preview dialog has three main tabs: Options, File, and Animation.

In the Options tab **(Figure 75)**, reducing the number of colors can result in a dramatic decrease in file size. Just don't throw away too many colors, or your animation may look worse for wear. Reduce the number gradually, and then test the animation with player controls in the preview window.

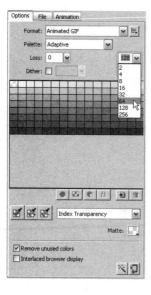

Figure 75 The Options tab has a lot of control over final file size.

Changing the Indexed Color palette can also have an effect on the file size, but some of the presets, like Windows, Mac, and Web 216, may alter the colors of your animation dramatically. Stick with Adaptive for the most flexibility. If you want the background color of your animation to be transparent, you can set Transparency to Index. This may further reduce your file size.

In the File tab, reducing the final image size or the area to be exported (you might have a lot of empty space on the canvas that isn't needed in the animation) will eliminate additional bytes.

The Animation tab provides another chance to alter the State Delay for the animation. Shift-click to select multiple frames, and then enter a value in the input box next to the little stopwatch.

Below the frame options are two little buttons that control looping of the animation.

Crop each state and Save differences between states are selected by default, and are two other optimization tools. Deselecting either of them will definitely increase your file size. The former will crop the animated objects so that only the changed pixels are kept. The latter compares the pixels in each frame and only saves the ones that change. This way you're not saving identical unchanged pixels over and over on each frame.

The last two buttons are wizard-style quick buttons. The Export Wizard guides you, step by step, through the optimization process. The Export to File Size only asks for one thing—the target size for your GIF. Specify how small you want the file, and it will chug away and create a file that comes in at or under your target size. This can be very helpful for creating animated banners, which have stringent file size limitations.

Creating a Flash Animation

After you have created an animation, you can also turn it into a Flash movie quite easily. Save your animation as a Fireworks PNG, so you retain editability. Then choose File > Save As and choose Adobe Flash SWF in the Save copy as drop-down menu.

SWF files are ready to drop into a Web page; they are completed movies and are not editable in Flash. If you want to bring in your animation as an editable file within Flash, see Techniques #95 and #96.

Disposal Method

The trash icon in the Animation tab symbolizes the disposal method for each frame. It's how you tell Fireworks what to do with a state after it has been displayed. You choose the method by clicking the trash can.

- **Unspecified.** Fireworks automatically selects the disposal method. If your animation is full frame, this setting creates the smallest possible file.

- **None.** The previous state is not disposed of. Each new state is loaded on top of the previous one. Previous states may show through transparent areas of the next state. Use this option to add a smaller object to the animation.

- **Restore to Background.** The current state is erased, and the area is restored to the Web page background color or image. Use this option if animated objects move above a transparent background.

- **Restore to Previous.** This option temporarily restores the state to the previous state's image. Use this option to move objects across the background image of a GIF animation.

CHAPTER ELEVEN

Improving Production Workflow

Working faster and smarter may be a cliché, but in the world of Web design it's also a goal. Don't mistake this work ethic with "cutting corners," which you do at your own risk. Working faster and smarter means taking advantage of the tools you have at hand to reduce time spent on repetitive tasks or just knowing your software well enough to produce quality work quickly.

#76 Changing Application Views on the Mac

The new Adobe interface gives applications a more consistent look across software and operating systems. However, if you prefer to use Fireworks as you did in version CS3, you can remove the integrated Application Frame by choosing Window and deselecting Use Application Frame. This puts all the panels and document window back into the more standard floating arrangement.

When Use Application Frame is selected, you get the single window as you would in Windows (**Figure 76a**). When deselected you get the traditional Macintosh layout with floating panels and document windows (**Figure 76b**).

Figure 76a By default, the standard OWL interface displays when you launch Fireworks.

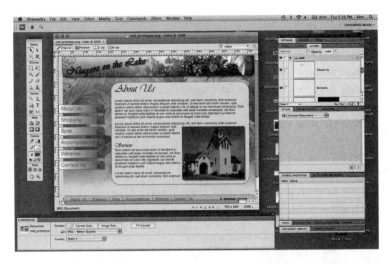

Figure 76b Mac users can opt to change to the traditional interface style if they prefer.

Floating or not, document windows can be tabbed with all documents in a single window, or each document can be displayed in its own window. Many Macintosh users prefer this layout (one document per window) because they use the Expose keyboard shortcuts to manage open windows.

#77 Using the Kuler Panel

Another new addition to Fireworks is the integration of a Kuler panel. Kuler is Adobe's online color theme sharing community and provides an easy way to kick-start your design process. You can even use the online Kuler service as a way to share color themes with members of your design team or with the worldwide Adobe design community.

To launch the Kuler panel, select Window > Extensions > Kuler.

In the Browse panel you can use, edit, or search for color themes from the Kuler Web site. If you select a color theme, a small triangle appears to the right of the theme name. Mousing over the triangle displays the theme name, ranking, creation date, and number of downloads. Click the triangle to open a context menu (**Figure 77a**) where you can choose to edit the theme, add it to the Swatches panel, or view the theme online.

Figure 77a Each theme has a context menu.

At the bottom of the Browse panel are the main Kuler controls (**Figure 77b**), which allow you to flip back and forth through themes, refresh the theme list, edit a selected theme in the Create panel, or add the current theme to the Swatches panel.

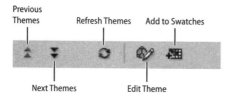

Figure 77b Controls for the Kuler Browse panel.

Switch to the Create panel and you're presented with a variety of color editing options: color harmony rules, a color wheel, theme swatches, RGB sliders, and even a hexadecimal input field where you can change the hex value or copy it to the clipboard for use elsewhere. At the bottom of the Create panel (**Figure 77c**) are controls for saving a theme, adding it to the Swatches panel, or uploading it to the Kuler Web site.

Add to Swatches

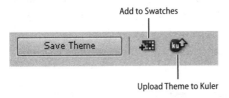

Upload Theme to Kuler

Figure 77c Controls for the Create panel.

If you find or create a series of colors you want to add to the Swatches panel, you can click the Add Theme to Swatches icon. The colors will be appended to the existing set of colors. This is quick and easy, but it may be more useful to create a custom swatch set. To do this, first open the Swatches panel and choose Clear Swatches from the panel options (**Figure 77d**). Then click the Add button in the Kuler panel. The Swatch panel populates with the theme colors. Choose Save Swatches from the panel options. You'll be prompted to name the .act file and choose a directory in which to save the file. This becomes a file you can share with others on your design team.

Figure 77d Clearing the swatches lets you create a custom swatch table filled only with the colors from the Kuler theme.

Free Sign Up

Uploading or accessing the Kuler Web site requires you to sign up. Sign up and membership to the Kuler community is free. Here is the Web site: http://kuler.adobe.com.

#**78** Naming Fireworks' Elements

When you are creating professional designs, it is so important to name the various elements of your design. You can name the following: pages, layers, sublayers, states, bitmap and vector objects, groups, text, Web slices, hotspots, and Web *sub*layers. These elements can either be named in their respective panels, in the Property Inspector, or both. The main Web layer on a page cannot be renamed.

When naming these elements, here are some guidelines to keep in mind:

- **Master Page and Page names** become HTML filenames when the pages are exported as HTML and Images or as CSS and Images. Name your pages using standard filenaming conventions to avoid navigation problems (no spaces or special characters in the names). You rename your pages by double-clicking on the default page name.

  You can rename a Master Page, but the moniker, "[Master Page]" cannot be altered.

- **Hierarchical layers** (layers and sublayers) make Fireworks much more compatible with Photoshop's layer-oriented structure. To name layers or sublayers, just double-click on the default name and add your new name. States are renamed in the same manner.

- **Bitmap, vector, and group objects, slices, and hotspots** can be renamed in the Layers panel or in the Property Inspector.

- **Text objects** are normally named using the first 20 characters of the text block, but you can replace that name with another that makes more sense. If, for example, you choose Commands > Text > Lorem Ipsum to create placement text for a sidebar area, double-click on the text name and rename it to something like **sidebar text**.

- **Slice names** become image filenames when the slices are exported, so use proper HTML naming conventions when naming slices. If you do not manually rename slices, Fireworks will auto name the slices based on their row/column/state position in an HTML table. These names—while unique—don't help you identify specific image slices.

- **Hotspot names** are not used for the images or the image map, but they can help you locate specific hotspots within the Web layer. The image map is named using the filename of the Fireworks document.

- **Web sublayers** are useful if you want to share navigation across multiple pages in your design. They can be renamed, but like hotspots this information is not carried over into a Web document.

Page Numbers

Pages are also auto numbered by Fireworks. As you add, remove, and change the order of pages, this number sequence updates to keep pages in order. You cannot change or turn off the auto numbering feature.

#79 Adding Structure to Your Documents

Creating a Master Page

You can only have one Master Page per file, and you can easily set *any* page in your design as the Master Page simply by choosing the Pages Options button or by right-clicking on a specific page and choosing Set as Master Page.

Sharing Layers

If you have a multipage design, sharing a layer (or layers) across pages can be a real time-saver. Unlike a Master Page, you can specify which pages get to share the layer. The location and visibility of a shared layer is maintained across all the pages it is applied to.

Using a shared layer makes it easy to apply changes to select pages at once. Once you edit the contents of a shared layer on any page, those changes are reflected on all the shared layer pages.

Fireworks calls the individual designs contained in a PNG file Pages and organizes them in the Pages panel. Pages can have different resolutions, canvas color, dimensions, layers, *and* Web layers. Using Pages is a great way to keep track of the design process. For example, rather than having multiple documents to represent various concepts or designs for a specific client, you can keep everything centralized with one Fireworks PNG file. Each design can be put on a distinct Page. You create a new empty Page by clicking the New Page icon in the Pages panel. You can then create, import, or paste objects into the new Page.

To maintain design consistency, consider dedicating one Page to specific client elements, such as color swatches and logos. This makes them easy to find.

Pages are also indispensable when it comes to creating interactive PDFs or HTML click-throughs, because each Page can represent a different Web page or PDF page.

Once you have established elements that won't change location from page to page, it's time to consider a Master Page. The Master Page is most useful for elements that have a common size and position in all pages. A header graphic and top navigation are good candidates for use in a Master Page because they will naturally stay at the top of the page in all cases. Elements such as a footer may not work on a Master Page, because your mock-up page lengths may vary. Much like shared layers, using a Master Page keeps your workflow simple and makes it easy to update common objects.

Multiple objects and sublayers can be placed in a single layer. You add layers and sublayers using the icons at the bottom of the Layers panel. You can change the order of layers or move a sublayer out of a main layer by dragging the layer within the Layers panel.

Keep related objects within the same main layer. Everyone knows how important it is to set up a navigational—and structural—hierarchy within a Web site. Well, complex designs can benefit from this manner of thinking as well.

Locking layers, sublayers, or objects can be useful as well to avoid inadvertently editing or moving an object. Click the lock icon to lock or unlock layers or objects.

You can use the Layers panel to control the visibility of objects and layers on the canvas. This can help you see how your project is progressing, simplify the layout, or see how certain elements interact with others. This feature is cascading in that hiding a layer hides *everything* in that layer, whether it was visible or not. When an object or layer is hidden in the Layers panel, it does not appear on the canvas, so it cannot be inadvertently changed or selected.

When to Use Sublayers

There are several reasons to use sublayers in your designs. They can help organize and simplify the Layers panel. With objects placed in sublayers rather than just sitting in a single layer, you can compress the layer stack and still recognize the contents by the sublayer name. Naming sublayers is important so collapsed layers and sublayers remain identifiable.

You can group layers that have related content. For example, you might have a main layer arrangement that mimics a Web page design. There could be header, content, and footer layers. Within the content layer, there could be a sidebar sublayer for navigation or teaser photos. Or you may have three sublayers that represent a three-column design.

In addition, using sublayers can make your designs more compatible with Photoshop, because Photoshop works with hierarchical layers as an organizational mechanism.

Seamless Integration with Photoshop

Photoshop and Fireworks layers and layer groups remain intact in PSD format. To maintain this layer structure in Photoshop, a file must be saved as a PSD.

Power Dragging

If you want to lock or hide multiple layers simultaneously, click and drag down the lock or eye column within the Layers panel or use the Layer Options panel.

Single Layer Editing

Single Layer Editing (available from the Layers panel Options menu) protects objects on all but the active layer from unwanted selection or changes. By default, this feature is turned *off* in Fireworks. The result is that on the canvas you can click on *any* object and select it regardless of the currently active layer. Enabling this feature means that you must choose the layer you want to work on by selecting it in the Layers panel.

#80 Site Prototyping— The Basics

Using the workflow techniques discussed in this chapter, let's create a simple Web site prototype.

1. Create a new document. A typical starting size for a Web page design is about 760 pixels wide by 420 pixels high. This takes into account how a fixed width page design will fit within a browser viewport with minimal horizontal scrolling when the viewer's monitor is set to 800×600 resolution.

2. Set a canvas color for the design.

3. Create a new layer and call it **common**.

4. To keep things simple, draw a rounded rectangle that is 740 pixels wide by 100 pixels high. Use Smart Guides to position the shape near the top and centered side to side. Name this object **header** (**Figure 80a**).

Figure 80a Even when creating simple mock-ups, naming objects is important.

5. Locate the Pages panel and right-click on this page. Select Set as Master Page. Rename the Master Page to **Main Design**.

6. Click the New Page icon in the Pages panel. The new page is created with all the features of the Master Page. Name this page **template**.

7. Create three new layers on this page. Name them **two column**, **three column**, and **footer**. Add two rectangles to the two column layer, three to the three column layer, and a similar rounded rectangle that is 740×30 pixels to the lower part of the footer layer. You may want to hide the layers as you build your columns, so they are easier to see.

Name each rectangle appropriately (column 1, column 2, etc.). The Layers panel should resemble **Figure 80b**.

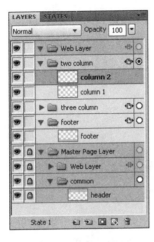

Figure 80b Multiple layers set up in the newly created "template" page. Note that the objects from the Master Page are visible but locked.

8. Create two more pages in the same way you created the first new page. Notice that only the elements from the Master Page are present in the new pages. Name the pages **index** and **about**. Yes, not terribly original, but work with me here!

9. Go back to the template page and select the two column layer. Choose Share Layer to Pages from the Layers panel Options menu. When the dialog appears, select the index page and click the Add button (**Figure 80c**). Click OK. Select the three column layer and choose Share Layer to Pages again. This time select the about page, click Add, and then click OK. Finally, select the footer layer and share this layer to *both* pages.

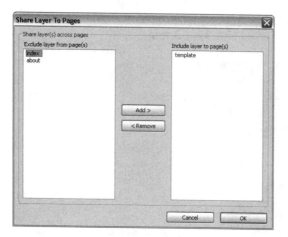

Figure 80c You have complete control over which pages you share to any given layer.

Now for the test: Select the index page from the Pages panel. You should see a two-column design. Select the about page, and the three column design should display.

In a few short minutes, you have created a simple mock-up design that utilizes Pages, shared layers, and a Master Page. Chapter 12 takes these basic concepts even further.

CHAPTER TWELVE

Designing Interfaces

Fireworks is uniquely placed in the Adobe product line as a graphical, rapid-prototyping tool. With a multitude of features, such as Pages, Web Layers, Component Symbols, interactive layout features (Smart Guides and Tooltips) and its ability to switch seamlessly from vector to bitmap graphic editing, Fireworks is an ideal application to use for mocking up Web page and application designs.

In this chapter you'll take a closer look at many of these tools. As you read this chapter, remember that Fireworks is an excellent graphics editor; it is not designed to be, nor should you expect it to be, an HTML Web page editor.

#81 Working with Pages

The Pages feature in Fireworks gives you lots of control and flexibility over your documents. In the past, building mock-ups meant you either had a series of separate files or you were constantly toggling layers and states on and off, just to see the different page designs. Pages also opens the door to creating interactive HTML and PDF mock-ups, and even a Flash-based slide show demo, further expanding your delivery options for the client.

Creating, deleting, sorting, and naming pages all occur within the Pages panel (**Figure 81a**). Let's explore this panel more deeply.

Figure 81a The Pages panel let's you select, rename, create, and delete pages.

Every document opened in Fireworks consists of at least one page, including new, empty documents. If you want to add a new page, click the New/Duplicate Page icon at the bottom of the panel.

You can easily rename pages by double-clicking on the default page name (Page 1, Page 2, etc.) and typing in a new name. Renaming as well as other options can also be accessed in a context menu (**Figure 81b**).

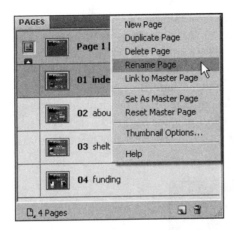

Figure 81b Options such as renaming a page or resetting a Master Page can be accessed in a context menu.

Just to the left of the page name is another Fireworks automatic feature—page numbering. As you add pages or change their order in the panel, this auto numbering feature updates, so the pages are always in numerical order. This feature cannot be edited or turned off.

A Master Page is a good place to add elements that will be common to all pages in a design, such as a header graphic for a Web page design. You can only have one Master Page per Fireworks document. Any elements you add to a Master Page (layers, graphics, Web elements) will be shared to all pages in the document and placed in exactly the same physical location on each page.

You can create a Master Page in a couple of ways:

- Right-click/Control + click an existing page and choose Set as Master Page.

- Select a page in the Pages panel and choose Set as Master Page from the Options menu.

If you create a Master Page, it will always reside at the top of the Pages panel and be identified as [Master Page].

You can just as easily turn a Master Page back into a regular page by using either of the same methods just mentioned, but instead select Reset Master Page.

You can access additional Page functions by right-clicking/Control-clicking on a single page or by clicking on the Pages panel options in the upper-right corner of the panel.

#82 Duplicating Pages

Most Web sites and applications have a similar look from page to page or screen to screen. For example, let's say you have designed a home page for a Web site. The header, footer, and overall look on subsequent pages will be the same, but page content will change. The site might switch from a two-column design to a three-column design.

If you are making design alterations to a page but don't want to damage or make changes to the original, drag the page to the New/Duplicate Page icon to create a duplicate page. You can also duplicate a page via a context menu (**Figure 82**).

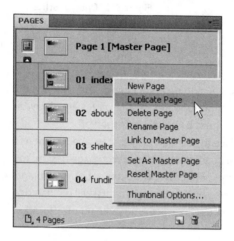

Figure 82 You can create a new or duplicate a page by right-clicking/Control+click on an existing page and choosing the desired option.

By duplicating an existing page design, you can speed up the mock-up process; just drag a current page to the New/Duplicate page icon. Once created, you can keep any common elements on this new page and delete or edit any content-specific elements.

#**83** Using Multiple Web Layers

The Web layer is where all interactive elements, such as hotspots and slices, are placed (**Figure 83**).

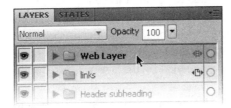

Figure 83 The Web layer is found at the top of each player stack on each page. You don't have to use it, but you cannot delete it from the document either.

Each Fireworks page, including the Master Page, supports its own interactive Web layer. This is key to the flexibility and power of Fireworks as a prototyping tool. As you create new pages, Fireworks adds a Web layer and a single empty image layer to the new page. This means you can have different interactive elements on each page, even in the same physical location as other pages.

Where this can come in very handy is if you need to slice a design differently for different uses. Prior to CS versions of Fireworks, you only had one page to work with, which meant that creating slices for different purposes was quite problematic because you could find yourself overlapping slices or having to turn slices on or off for each export. Now you can simply duplicate a page and slice it differently on the duplicate. As long as the slices have different names, the graphics from each page should export properly.

#84 Sharing Layers Across Pages

Designing for Client Approval and Speedy Deployment

Fireworks gives you many options for delivering your ideas or prototype designs to the client:

- **File > Send to Email** converts the existing design to either a JPEG or Fireworks PNG and inserts it as an attachment in an email message.

- **File > Export > HTML and Images** exports your design as an interactive HTML prototype.

- **File > Export > Adobe PDF** lets you export a secure standard or interactive PDF, enabling your client to print, review, and comment on the designs without the need for an Internet connection.

- **Commands > Demo Current Document** creates a Flash-based slide show of each page in the document. You choose which pages are added to the presentation using the features dialog.

- **Commands > Create AIR Package** lets you generate an interactive AIR prototype of a mocked up application.

The Pages and Layers features of Fireworks add a great deal of time-saving functionality to your workflow. Picture a design with identical navigation on each page. Any time you needed to update this content (changing its location or the objects), you would have to perform the same actions on each page. Rather than waste time doing this, consider placing these objects in the same layer and sharing this layer to other pages. When you share layers across pages, any change made in the layer will be reflected on all the sharing pages.

To share a layer, select it in the Layers panel and choose Share Layer to Pages from the Layers panel Options (**Figure 84**). A dialog opens. On the left are all the pages not yet sharing the layer; on the right are the pages sharing the layer. Simply select pages on the left and click the Add button to enable sharing of all the elements in that specific layer. Click OK when you are done. If you switch between pages, you will see that the layer has been added to each page you chose, and it is identified by a different color in the layer bar and by a small icon that looks like a page icon with a triangle on either side of it.

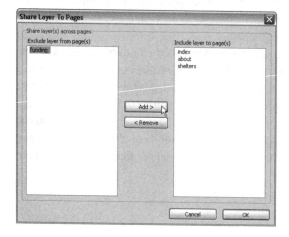

Figure 84 The Share Layers to Pages dialog lets you share or remove sharing of a layer to any Fireworks page in the current document, giving you more specific control than you would have if the layer was placed on the Master Page.

Take a minute to change the position or content of any object in this layer (you can do this from any of the pages sharing the layer). Check your other pages to see that they have been updated with the change. This is just another way to work smarter, not harder.

#85 Creating HTML Mock-ups

Creating an interactive mock-up at its simplest requires the use of Pages, regular layers, and a Web layer. As discussed in other techniques, you create interactive elements in Fireworks by using hotspots or slices. You can add proper URLs to both Web objects, or you can use them to link to other pages in your design using the Link box in the Property Inspector. If you have a multipage design and want to create a link from one page to another, draw a hotspot over part of your design. In the Property Inspector, click the Link box at the bottom of the Link drop-down menu; you will see Web pages that use the same names as the ones listed in the Pages panel.

When you select the page from the drop-down menu, your link is created (**Figure 85**).

You can also use image slices if you want to create a rollover effect as well as create a link. Check out Technique #45 for more on this process.

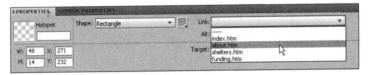

Figure 85 Links can be added manually to the Link box or selected from the list of pages in the drop-down menu.

What Do I Slice?

There is rarely any need to slice up an entire Web page design. Elements such as regular text or form components do not require slicing in a prototype design. Only slice elements destined to be images, such as rollover images, images that will appear inline in the HTML (individual photos in a design for example), perhaps a header image, stylized text (text on a path or text using a nonstandard font or other special treatment), and background images. Quite often, repeating background images are sliced into a small piece, which can be tiled in your Web page design, reducing the overall file size of the Web page.

Prototype, Not Production

When you export as HTML and Images, Fireworks generates all the HTML and JavaScript necessary to reproduce your design faithfully. Keep in mind that Fireworks does this by slicing up your entire design and converting everything—including text—into graphics and then assembling these sliced images into a very rigid HTML table-based design. While suitable for testing and feedback, it is not recommended you use this HTML for your final production Web site. The table created by Fireworks can easily be "broken" if you remove images from it or try to replace the bitmap text images with true HTML text.

When Can I Use Fireworks HTML in My Real Web Site?

If you are creating a series of navigation buttons, the resulting HTML from this segment of your design may not differ greatly from what you would do in Fireworks or another Web editor. You will need to place the navigation bar on its own page so that nothing else is exported with it. You may even be able to use the simplest table option (Single Table, No Spacers). The benefit of doing so is that Fireworks also includes any hotspot (image map) code and any JavaScript for image rollovers.

Fireworks HTML can also be useful when you choose the CSS and Images export option. It will generate standards-based CSS for the page layout, but this option will not include the HTML for items such as image maps or rollovers.

Still, the most common practice among design professionals is to use Fireworks for creating images and Dreamweaver and CSS for adding interactivity.

#86 Using Hotspots for Mock-up Navigation

To create an interactive design using hotspots, follow these steps:

1. Create a new Fireworks document.

2. Use the Text tool to create three labels for text hyperlinks—Home, About, Contact Us—and align them vertically.

3. Draw a hotspot over each of these text areas, and then take a look at your Web layer in the Layers panel. You should see the three hotspots.

4. Create a duplicate page using the Pages panel. Note that the Web layer in this page also has the same hotspots.

5. Just to the right of the About link, add three more text areas, simulating a flyout menu.

6. Add hotspots to those text areas.

7. Switch back to Page 1 and check out the Web layer. You won't see those new hotspots; they are only part of the second page.

In much the same manner, you can mock up an accordion style menu.

1. Create another duplicate of Page 1.

2. On this new page, move the text area for Contact Us lower on the canvas.

3. Move the hotspot for Contact Us as well, so it once again covers the text.

4. Use the newly created space to add in links for the About label.

5. Add hotspots to those text areas.

As you switch between pages, you will again see that the Web layer remains independent on each page.

#**87** Sharing Web Layers

Much like sharing standard Layers, you can also share Web layers among pages. There is a trick to this, however. The main Web Layer of a page cannot be shared or even renamed. But you can create a Web *sublayer*, and that layer can be shared like any normal layer in a Fireworks design.

This can save you time if you have common navigation elements on all or several pages of your design. Like a shared layer, a shared Web layer lets you update all the attributes of the layer in one place and update the pages where the Web layer is shared.

To create a Web sublayer:

1. Select the Web layer, and then click the New Sublayer icon at the bottom of the Layers panel (**Figure 87**).

2. With that sublayer active, add in your interactive Web elements.

3. Select Share Layer to Pages from the Layers panel Options menu.

4. Choose which pages you want to share the Web layer with, and then click OK.

Switching through your pages will show you that the Web elements are present on each page.

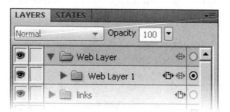

Figure 87 A Web sublayer appears below the main Web layer and is slightly indented at the left.

#**88** Previewing Your Mock-up

You can preview your mock-up in one of two ways:

- Choose the Preview view in the document window (**Figure 88a**). Roll-overs will function and so will links to other pages within the document.

Figure 88a The Preview views are found above the canvas.

- For a more realistic preview, choose File > Preview in Browser > Preview All Pages in Browser (**Figure 88b**). Fireworks will create temporary Web pages of all the pages in your document and launch the current page within a Web browser. You can even choose more than one browser to check your design by setting Primary and Secondary browsers. If you have a live Internet connection, your links to external Web sites will function just as well as your links to pages within the Fireworks PNG file.

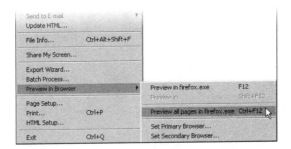

Figure 88b Preview All Pages in Browser will launch your default Web browser so you can test your entire design. While not a perfect rendition due to browser chrome, you could also use this step to preview an interactive AIR mock-up.

Preview in Browser for HTML Prototypes

The Preview in Browser option is only intended for HTML prototypes, so you'll need to make sure you've chosen HTML and Images as your export type before you successfully preview. Ironically, this means you actually have to export the mock-up once to lock in those options.

#89 Exporting an Interactive Mock-up

By using a combination of slices and hotspots, you can create a realistic and interactive mock-up of a functional Web site. This step in the Web design process can be invaluable; it gives your client one more opportunity to review the site's design and flow before you spend precious time coding the final HTML pages. Let's look at how to turn your multipage Fireworks file into an interactive mock-up.

Fireworks creates this mock-up prototype style when you choose Export > HTML and Images.

When the Export dialog appears, choose HTML and Images from the Export drop-down menu, and then choose Export HTML file from the HTML menu and Export Slices from the Slice menu (**Figure 89**). Also ensure that the Include Areas without Slices option is selected and the Current Page Only option is deselected.

Optionally, you can tell Fireworks to place the images in a subfolder. You can browse for this folder (it should be in the same folder as the one you are exporting to), or Fireworks will automatically generate a folder called "images" for you.

For further control, you can click the Options button. For more details, see the sidebar, "HTML Options."

Figure 89 The Export dialog sets a variety of export options, including HTML and Images.

HTML Options

- **General** controls aspects about the HTML document, such as the HTML style and file extension to use.

- **Table** controls the HTML table Fireworks creates. Choose from Nested Table, No Spacers; Single Table, No Spacers; or 1-Pixel transparent spacer. This last choice is the most rigid of the three but produces an exact match to your Fireworks design. The Nested Table, No Spacers falls a close second in its HTML fragility, but the HTML for the table may be less complex. Single Table, No Spacers is the least complex, but your Web page may display differently than the Fireworks document. For a prototype, try Nested Table to see if the Web page matches your PNG file. If so, use it, remembering that this is just for feedback purposes.

- **Document Specific** controls how Fireworks names the files from unnamed Web slices, pop-up menus, and unsliced areas. With auto named slices, Fireworks ensures that each image slice is unique, so that no files are overwritten during the export. You can also input generic ALT text so that each image receives a basic ALT description.

#90 Exporting a CSS-based Layout

What is a Div Tag?

Div is short for division. In HTML this tag is a generic container tag for holding other content. It is used extensively in CSS-based designs to control the position of content in a Web page design.

CSS is all the rage, and there are a lot of good reasons for this. Separating content from presentation, easier to maintain Web pages, and global control over a site's look and feel *from a single document* are the most common reasons for turning to CSS-based Web page layouts. Well structured CSS-based pages are also critical to delivering content to mobile devices such as the iPhone and Blackberry. Fireworks offers an export option called CSS and Images. Let's look at this feature and the thought process behind using it.

When you're designing your layout, keep in mind the whole concept of columns and rows. Even though the HTML file won't use a table, Fireworks will do a better job at setting up the CSS and HTML div tags if your design has distinct areas where, in essence, you could draw a box around specific content.

If you have overlap conflicts (a text area overlapping an image slice for example), Fireworks will still generate a CSS layout, but it will be an absolutely positioned layout. This type of CSS layout is still valid but is much less flexible in terms of how you can edit the HTML file and how it will display.

When you slice images, you can choose between foreground and background image slices in the Property Inspector. Generally, unless the image is necessary for the comprehension of the page content, background slices are recommended. Small slices used as repeating background images also produce a smaller, faster-loading page. Background slices do not require alternate text descriptions either. Text, unless it's stylized, should not be sliced if you plan to export with this option.

To export CSS and Images, choose File > Export, and then choose CSS and Images from the Export drop-down menu. You can also opt to place the images in a subfolder.

For additional control, click the Options button. You can then choose to export the CSS as an external file. If left deselected, Fireworks will embed the CSS in the head of the HTML document. You can also set a background image and the page alignment.

Additional tweaking can be done with Dreamweaver or the HTML editor of your choice. Because this is the first time this feature has been available natively within Fireworks, I would not be surprised to see further updates to the CSS and Images export as the application evolves.

CSS Resources

This book is not the place to discuss the concepts of CSS in any detail. If this is an area you are unfamiliar with, you should read up on CSS and more specifically CSS Positioning (CSS-P).

Many resources are available for learning about CSS. Here is a short list:

- http://meyerweb.com/eric/css/
- http://www.communitymx.com (free and commercial tutorials)
- http://www.alisapart.com
- http://www.w3schools.com
- http://www.lynda.com
- http://www.positioniseverything.net/
- http://www.brainjar.com/

Understanding How Fireworks Creates CSS Designs

The goal of the export script is to produce a relatively positioned CSS-based layout, which is more accessible and gives you more flexibility in editing the final layout in a Web editor, such as Dreamweaver. Think of the CSS that Fireworks produces as a means to reduce production time and "get started" with your CSS-based design.

The CSS and Images export script only exports the currently visible page in your design, not the hotspots or rollover states. These must be added into the HTML page manually, and in the case of rollover states, exported manually from Fireworks.

Fireworks exports unsliced text areas as true HTML text. So you can literally open the page in a Web editor and change text right in the document!

HTML symbols (heading1–6, link and form elements) export as true HTML with the appropriate coding, and in the case of the link component, even the URL.

On export, Fireworks tries to place text in logical HTML div containers. Sliced images will also be placed in divs. Unsliced images will be ignored. Images will be exported as either foreground or background images, depending on what you have chosen.

#91 Creating an AIR Prototype

While Fireworks cannot create a fully functioning Adobe Integrated Runtime (AIR) application, you can create an AIR prototype that will have interactive elements that allow you to preview how the design will look. An AIR prototype can include text, graphics, rollovers, hotspots, and clickable events. This is an opportunity to have the client "test-drive" the design and functionality of an AIR application before any time is spent on the coding side.

Most of the techniques used in creating an HTML mock-up can be applied to creating an AIR prototype.

To create the prototype, select Commands > Create Air Package and complete the options in the dialog (**Figure 91**).

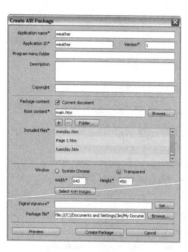

Figure 91 The Create AIR Package dialog must be completed to create an AIR prototype. You can also preview your prototype from this dialog.

- **Application name.** Specify the name that appears on installation screens when users install the application.

- **Application ID (required).** Enter a unique ID for your application. Don't use spaces or special characters in the ID.

- **Version (required).** Specify a version number for your application.

- **Program menu folder (Windows only).** Specify the folder in the Windows Start menu where you want the shortcut to the application created.

- **Description.** Add a description of the application to display when the user installs the application.

- **Copyright (Mac only).** Include copyright information that is displayed in the About information for Adobe AIR applications installed on Mac OS.

- **Package content.** Select Current document to automatically select the folder from which the files are included. The resulting list will be simpler if your PNG file is in its own folder rather than, for example, your desktop or main documents folder.

- **Root content.** Browse to select the page that appears as the root content (starting screen of the prototype). If you selected Current document, the root content is automatically set.

- **Included files.** Specify the files or folders to include in your application. You can add HTML and CSS files, image files, and JavaScript library files. Click the Plus (+) button to add files and click Folder to add folders. To delete a file or folder from your list, select the file or folder and click the Minus (–) button. The files or folders you include in the Adobe AIR package must be in the root content folder.

- **System Chrome and Transparent.** System chrome surrounds the prototype with the standard window control of the operating system. Transparent lets you use your own custom chrome instead.

- **Width and Height.** Specify the dimensions of your application window in pixels when it opens. Depending on your page sizes, you may need to increase the dimensions slightly to avoid scroll bars from appearing.

- **Select Icon Images.** You can select custom images for the application icons. Select the folder for each icon size and select the image file you want to use. Only PNG files are supported for application icon images.

- **Digital signature (required).** For more information, see the sidebar, "Creating a Digital Signature."

- **Package file (required).** Specify the folder to save the new application installer (.air file). The default location is the site root. Click the Browse button to select a different location. The default filename is based on the site name with an .air extension added to it.

Creating a Digital Signature

All Adobe AIR applications require a digital signature and can't be installed without one.

In the Create AIR Package dialog, click the Set button next to the Digital Signature option. In the Digital Signature dialog, do one of the following:

- To sign an application with a prepurchased digital certificate, click the Browse button, select the certificate, enter the corresponding password, and click OK.

- To create your own self-signed digital certificate, click the Create button and complete the dialog. The certificate Key Type option refers to the level of security of the certificate: 1024-RSA uses a 1024-bit key (less secure) and 2048-RSA uses a 2048-bit key (more secure).

When you're finished, click Create. Then enter the corresponding password in the Digital Signature dialog and click OK.

Add Your Own Icons

You can add your own custom application icons by clicking on the "Add Icons" button in the Create AIR Package dialog. You will be prompted to browse for the existing graphics.

Note the graphics must be specific dimensions, and you must have a graphic for each icon size. You can't opt for just a 48x48 pixel icon.

The graphics must be PNG files and they must also be located in the Package Content folder.

Before you create the package, you can preview the prototype by selecting the Preview button. If you are happy with the preview, select Create Package. Fireworks will export the final AIR executable to the folder designated in the Package file input box (Figure 91).

Once the export is complete, locate the AIR application mock-up file. It will have a .air file extension. Double click on the icon to launch the installer. This is the only file you need if you want to share the prototype with other team members or the client.

AIR Mouse Events

You can attach specific mouse events to hotspots or slices in your AIR mock-up. Select the Web element (slice or hotspot), and then choose Commands > AIR Mouse Events. You can choose from four options:

- **Close.** Closes the application.
- **Drag.** You pick a Web element that lets the user drag the application around the desktop.
- **Maximize.** Maximizes the application.
- **Minimize.** Minimizes the application.

CHAPTER THIRTEEN

Fitting Fireworks into the Design Workflow

Nobody designs in a vacuum. For screen-based graphics, Fireworks is an ideal main application, but it can also act as a "hub," accepting files from several different sources and also outputting files in a variety of formats. This chapter explores how Fireworks fits in with other applications such as Bridge, Dreamweaver, Photoshop, and Flash, as well as application technologies such as Adobe Flex and a new application code named "Thermo."

#92 Working with Metadata

You can add metadata to many types of files within Fireworks, including PNG, GIF, JPEG, Photoshop (PSD), and TIFF files. This allows you to share information about the author, copyright, and keywords with users of other Adobe applications.

To add or edit metadata, select File > File Info to launch the Adobe XMP (Extensible Meta Data Platform) window. Several industry or file-specific tabs are available, but the most common is the Description tab. None of the fields are mandatory; simply fill in those you want to use (**Figure 92**).

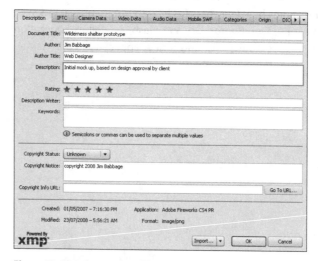

Figure 92 Metadata can be added to a variety of file types and can even be saved as a template for use on other files.

Even though the XMP window is not specifically meant as a project management tool, I often also include basic information about the project file and even the client name in the Description field.

Creating a Metadata Template

You can create basic metadata templates to use for any appropriate file. Add the basic information you would normally use for any project (author, author title, copyright), and then choose Export (from the Import drop-down menu). The Metadata Templates folder opens. Name the file and click Save.

Next time you start a new document or open one that doesn't contain metadata you can select Import and choose the template you want to use.

#93 Using Fireworks' Tools in Bridge

Bridge can kick-start some of Fireworks' more automated commands, much like it can for Photoshop, Illustrator, and InDesign. These commands are also accessible within Fireworks. The advantage to accessing these commands from Bridge is that you can select specific files to apply the command to before running it.

To access these commands within Bridge, choose Tools > Fireworks. The most powerful of these commands is Batch Process (**Figure 93a**). You can use this main command to export, scale, and rename selected files; find and replace elements within selected Fireworks PNG files; or access many other commands. By choosing the Export command within the Batch Process window for example (**Figure 93b**), you can save files in a different format.

The other three commands available in the Tools menu will open the selected files in Fireworks and apply the command. You must manually save the files within Fireworks before you close them.

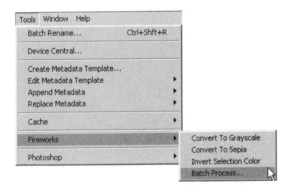

Figure 93a The Fireworks automated features found in Bridge represent some common commands found in Fireworks.

Figure 93b The Batch Process command lets you access many other automated commands within Fireworks, including custom commands you can create yourself.

#94 Integrating Fireworks with Photoshop

Various techniques in this book have discussed Photoshop integration (Techniques #16 and #23 specifically), but for those of you who need to move between Fireworks and Photoshop, here are some things to consider.

When moving from Fireworks to Photoshop:

- **Do not open Fireworks PNG files in Photoshop.** Photoshop will flatten all aspects of the file. If you need to go to Photoshop, save your file as a Photoshop PSD file.

- **Use layers and sublayers to structure your design.** When saved as a PSD, Fireworks will convert this hierarchy into layer groups, maintaining visibility, lock status, and layer names. Objects within a layer or sublayer will be converted to layers.

- **Use Photoshop Live Effects rather than Fireworks Live Filters.** This guarantees support for the effects within Photoshop as Layer Styles.

- **Multiple pages are not supported in Photoshop.** If you have a multipage document, you'll need to select each page and export it as a separate PSD file.

- **Image slice dimensions and names are maintained in the Photoshop file.** But optimization settings are not maintained in the Photoshop file.

As noted in Techniques #16 and #23, Fireworks has some pretty robust controls when opening or importing a Photoshop document. That said, here are some other points to consider when moving from Photoshop to Fireworks:

- **Fireworks does not support Smart Objects.** They will import as flattened graphical objects.

- **Fireworks does not support adjustment layers.** Adjustment layers will be discarded unless you choose Flatten Photoshop Layers to Single Image. This will retain the effect, but the file will be flattened so those effects will not be editable.

- **Fireworks retains image slices and slice names created in Photoshop.** Optimize settings are not retained.

Using Photoshop Filters and Plug-ins

Third-party plug-ins and filters for Photoshop 5.5 and earlier versions are supported in Fireworks.

1. Choose Edit > Preferences (Windows) or Fireworks > Preferences (Mac OS).

2. Click the Plug-Ins category and select Photoshop Plug-Ins.

3. The Select a Folder (Windows) or Choose a Folder (Mac OS) dialog opens.

4. Navigate to the folder where the Photoshop or other filters and plug-ins are installed and click Select (Windows) or Choose (Mac OS).

5. Click OK to close the Preferences dialog.

6. Restart Fireworks.

Native Photoshop 5.5 filters are also supported on Windows. However, you may need to edit the Disabled plugins.txt file found in the configuration folder within the Fireworks CS4 application folder. If you do so, be sure to make a copy of the .txt file.

#95 Prototyping Flash Interfaces with Fireworks

Importing Fireworks Files to Flash

Here are a few factors to consider when importing Fireworks files to Flash:

- **HTML.** Pop-up menu code is not supported by Flash. Likewise, interactivity and button behaviors are not imported to Flash either.

- **Vectors and text.** Flash does not support all the special effects, fills, and strokes available in Fireworks. When you import a Fireworks PNG file and choose to keep the file as editable as possible, these features may look different. Flash supports only solid fills, gradient fills (except the contour gradient), and basic strokes.

- **Bitmaps.** When Fireworks graphics are imported or copied and pasted into Flash, some attributes are lost, such as Live Filters and textures.

- **Graphic symbols.** Graphic symbols with 9-slice scaling are supported in Flash, but 9-slice scaling is not maintained for animation symbols.

Fireworks can be used as a prototyping and design tool for creating Flash interfaces just as it can for HTML and other applications. Since the bitmap editing tools in Fireworks are significantly more robust than those native to Flash, Fireworks is a great place to start when you need to design a Flash interface. You can employ many of Fireworks' filters and effects to create your Flash design, and then export individual items or the entire prototype for use in Flash.

When working between Fireworks and Flash, the most efficient way to maintain design integrity is through the use of symbols. When you convert an object into a symbol in Fireworks, you can import it directly into a Flash file. The symbol will retain layers and its name, and be placed into the Flash Library for use in your design. If you choose to keep your vectors editable in the Import dialog that Flash displays, you will even be able to modify an object originally drawn in Fireworks by double clicking the symbol until you drill down to its editable form.

Vector masks (even with simple gradient fills) are also supported and remain editable within Flash.

You can also use the bitmap tools in Fireworks to select part of a bitmap, and then copy and paste the selection into Flash. Be warned though: Flash will create a generic PNG filename for the pasted selection, and you will not have any round-trip editing capability. You'll need to copy the graphic back to Fireworks to edit it.

#96 Importing to Flash

You have a lot of options if you plan to export your artwork to Flash. In most cases, exporting your artwork is as simple as just saving your file as a Fireworks PNG, JPEG, GIF, SWF, or flat PNG file, and then choosing File > Import in Flash

Copying and pasting symbols is an option if you want specific elements within a design brought into Flash.

Flash also has excellent support for Fireworks PNG files (**Figure 96**). You can import an entire Fireworks file into Flash, and all symbols and layer states are placed into the Library automatically. Once all the objects are in place you can continue with your Flash design work, adding animation and interactive elements through the Flash working environment.

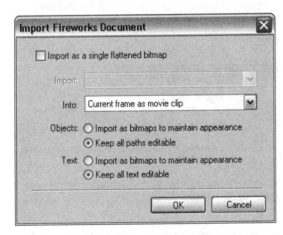

Figure 96 The Import dialog displays when you import a Fireworks PNG file into the Flash Library or to the Flash Stage.

Fireworks vectors, bitmaps, animations, and multistate button graphics can also be imported into Flash.

If you import a flat image file (GIF, JPEG, standard PNG file) to Flash, you can easily edit and update the file by right-clicking/Control-clicking the graphic file in the Document Library panel. Choose Edit with Fireworks and, if you want to edit the original Fireworks PNG file, choose Yes in the Find Source box to locate the original PNG file for your Fireworks graphic. Then click Open.

When you are finished editing, click Done in the Fireworks document window. The PNG file will be saved, and the file will be updated in Flash.

#97 Round-trip Editing Between Dreamweaver and Fireworks

Dreamweaver and Fireworks have always been tightly integrated. In fact, Fireworks may have even been responsible for coining the phrase "round-trip editing." This process refers to the ability to edit the images in a Fireworks generated HTML table right from Dreamweaver (**Figure 97a**). The beauty of this editing cycle is that as soon as you are done editing in Fireworks, the Web page and content are automatically saved and updated in Dreamweaver. If you think about the HTML prototypes discussed in Chapter 12, "Designing Interfaces," you can see where this feature might be quite useful after a client has reviewed an online mock-up.

To take advantage of round-trip editing, click anywhere inside the HTML table within Dreamweaver. Then in the Tag Selector, click on the main table tag. The Property Inspector will update to show you the path to the source PNG file, and beside it an Edit button will appear with the Fireworks icon inside it.

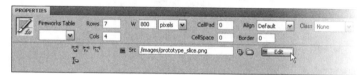

Figure 97a Fireworks and Dreamweaver integration make it easy to edit a Fireworks design right from Dreamweaver.

Click the Edit button and Dreamweaver will launch Fireworks and open the source PNG file for you. If Fireworks can't find the PNG file, it will prompt you to browse for the file.

When the file opens, you'll see near the upper-left corner a button labeled Done and the status message, "Editing from Dreamweaver" (**Figure 97b**).

Figure 97b Clicking Done resaves the PNG file, updates the HTML, and brings you back to Dreamweaver.

Make your changes to the file in Fireworks. You can edit images and even move them around, but try not go crazy repositioning elements because it can greatly affect the HTML table. Then, rather than saving the PNG, click the Done button. Fireworks saves the PNG, and Dreamweaver appears with the updated HTML and graphics in place.

#98 Copy and Paste to Dreamweaver

You can copy and paste selected objects or a bitmap selection right into Dreamweaver. Make your selection and choose Edit > Copy. Move to Dreamweaver, open the destination Web page, and select Edit > Paste. The Image Preview dialog (**Figure 98**) appears so you can choose a file format and optimization settings, as well as size the image and crop it. When you have made all your choices, click OK to add the image file to the Web page.

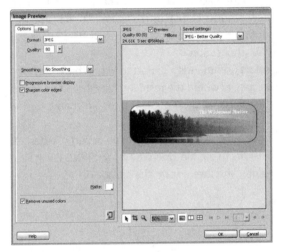

Figure 98 Pasting selected objects from Fireworks to Dreamweaver launches the Image Preview dialog, so you can convert the selected objects to a single, flattened, Web-ready graphic format.

Note
You can only make a bitmap selection if your objects are all bitmaps. If objects you want to copy include text or vectors, you must select them using the Pointer tool or select them in the Layers panel.

Editing Graphics in Dreamweaver

Changing the properties of an image within a Web page editing program is not usually recommended, but if you have Fireworks and Dreamweaver installed, you can take advantage of some basic bitmap editing without leaving Dreamweaver.

Simply choose an image in the Web page, The Properties inspector will give you several bitmap tools to use. You can optimize, scale, crop, lighten, darken, sharpen, or blur an image in the Dreamweaver workspace.

These changes are made directly to the selected image file, and will permanently alter the image.

#99 Using Fireworks with Flex or Thermo

What Is Thermo?

Thermo is the code name for a new Adobe product that focuses on making it easy for designers to create rich Internet application UIs. You can learn more about Thermo at http://labs. adobe.com/wiki/index.php/ Thermo.

If you are working with Flex developers or other programmers who create rich-media experiences, you may find that you need to export a Fireworks design or Fireworks objects in a format they can use. This format is called FXG, which is a graphics file format based on a subset of MXML (the XML-based programming language used by the Flex framework).

The FXG format can help you collaborate more efficiently with Flex developers or Thermo designers. You can create graphics using Fireworks CS4 and export them into this FXG format. The FXG file can then be used by tools such as the new product code named "Thermo" to develop rich Internet applications that run in a Web browser using the Flash Player or on the desktop as an AIR application.

To export in FXG, select Commands > Export to FXG. A browsing window opens so you can specify where the resulting files should be saved. A JavaScript dialog then appears, prompting you for a filename for the FXG file.

Thermo can then import the file for use as a design or part of a design.

If you need to make edits to the file, open the original PNG file in Fireworks, make your changes, and then export the file again.

#100 Creating Skins for Flex

You can skin Flex components (buttons, accordion menus, form elements, etc.) in Fireworks, and then export them for use in building Flex-based Web sites and application interfaces. "Skinning" is the term used for making Flex components visually appealing. Fireworks comes installed with a default Flex "skin," which you can modify to match the look and feel of a Flex application.

You access this default skin by selecting Commands > Flex Skinning > New Flex Skin. In the dialog (**Figure 100a**), choose to edit specific components (just the accordion menu for example) or the entire skin.

Figure 100a The New Flex Skin dialog lets you choose whether you want to create an entire new skin or just edit specific components.

The multiple component skin contains editable objects for all the Flex UI components, such as radio buttons, accordion menus, buttons, and the like (**Figure 100b**). You can edit the objects as you would any Fireworks object. Be careful to not rename any layer in the Layers panel, however, because these are named specifically to match Flex naming conventions

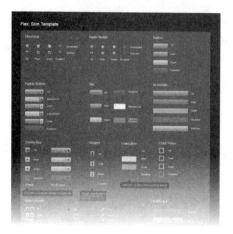

Figure 100b When you choose to create a new Flex skin for multiple components, Fireworks opens a complete PNG file containing all the common Flex components as editable objects, many of which you see in this figure.

Once you have styled the objects as desired, select Commands > Flex Skinning > Export Flex Skin. Browse to the folder where you want to save the objects. A JavaScript file will export all the elements using specific Flex filenames. When complete, you can import the objects into Flex or send the folder to the Flex designer.

Index